Who Do They Say I Am?:
The Vindication of Minister Louis Farrakhan

A never before seen compilation of a veritable Who's Who of Elected Officials, Celebrities, Journalists, Religious Leaders, Pastors, Professors and Organizations who testify to the Character, Impact and Immeasurable Value of

•The Honorable Minister Louis Farrakhan•

By Brother Demetric Muhammad

August 2013

Table of Contents

TABLE OF CONTENTS 3
FOREWORD 7
PREFACE 11
INTRODUCTION 24
WHAT DO THEY SAY ABOUT FARRAKHAN? 33

    FORMER GOVERNOR AND MAYOR, ED RENDELL 33
    ACTOR AND CELEBRITY BRUCE WILLIS 33
    RAPPER CHUCK D 34
    RAPPER NAS 34
    5 TERM MEMPHIS MAYOR WILLIE HERENTON 35
    CHICAGO TRIBUNE EDITORIAL PAGE EDITOR, DON WYCLIFF 36
    TRUMPET MAGAZINE EDITOR RHONDA MCKINNEY JONES 36
    REV. JEREMIAH A. WRIGHT 37
    FORMER ECONOMIC ADVISER TO PRES. RONALD REAGAN AND WALL STREET GURU, JUDE WANNISKI 37
    ACLC PRESIDENT ARCHBISHOP GEORGE A. STALLINGS 37
    TORAH JEWISH GROUP NETUREI KARTA 38
    FORMER U.S. REPRESENTATIVE AND HUD SECRETARY JACK KEMP 41
    FORMER EEOC CHAIRMAN AND U.S. SUPREME COURT JUSTICE CLARENCE THOMAS ... 41
    HIP-HOP MOGUL AND ENTREPRENEUR RUSSELL SIMMONS 42
    RAPPER 50 CENT 44
    R&B VOCALIST STEPHANIE MILLS 44
    REV. JESSE L. JACKSON SR. 44
    PROFESSOR MICHAEL ERIC DYSON 44
    ELMA LEWIS, FRIEND OF THE MINISTER'S MOTHER 45
    PASTOR OF ST. SABINA CHURCH AND COMMUNITY ACTIVIST FATHER MICHAEL PFLEGER 45
    JOURNALIST GREGORY KANE 45
    HAKI R. MADHUBUTI 47
    DR. CORNEL WEST 47
    ALICE WALKER 48
    SELWYN SEYFU HINDS 48
    RON DANIELS 48
    DR. CHARSHEE MCINTYRE AND DR. BARBARA SIZEMORE 49
    DR. GENEVA SMITHERMAN 49

JOURNALIST AND PUBLISHER OF EMERGE MAGAZINE GEORGE CURRY	50
JOURNALIST AND ACTIVIST KEVIN POWELL	50
MUSICIAN AND COMPOSER JAMES MTUME	50
ACTOR BERNIE CASEY	50
COLLEGE FRIEND CLARENCE "JEEP" JONES	51
BROTHER WAYNE GRICE	51
PRESIDENT BILL CLINTON	51
U.S. REPRESENTATIVE JAMES TRAFICANT	52
LAWANNA MAYFIELD	53
JEFFREY STEINBERG	54
KWEISI MFUME	55
ANDREW YOUNG	55
DEBRA HANANIA-FREEMAN	56
FREDRICK ALLEN	56
PROFESSOR DERRICK BELL	57
JOURNALIST CLARENCE PAGE	57
POET AND WRITER NIKKI GIOVANNI	57
SNOOP DOGG (LION) RAPPER/ACTOR	58
BOXING HEAVYWEIGHT CHAMPION MIKE TYSON	59
JOURNALIST AND WRITER FAHIZAH ALIM	60
DR. AMINAH MCCLOUD	62
IMAM WARITHUDEEN MOHAMMED	62
IMAM SIRAJ WAHHAJ	64
HENRY LOUIS GATES AND DR. C. ERIC LINCOLN	64
PROFESSOR ERNEST ALLEN JR.	65
DR. MICHAEL ERIC DYSON	66
RON NIXON	66
ROBERT MICHAEL FRANKLIN	67
SALIMMUWAKKIL	69
GWENDOLYN BROOKS	70
PROFESSOR DERRICK BELL	70
HENRY LOUIS GATES JR.	70
DANIEL K. TABOR, CITY COUNCILMAN	71
ROBERT A. JORDAN	71
BLACK ENTERTAINMENT TELEVISION	73
WYCLEF JEAN	74
ERYKAH BADU	74
MARY J. BLIGE	75
JOURNALIST ELLEN HUME	75

HARRY L. THOMAS, SR. 76
WILLIAM RASPBERRY 77
NATHAN MCCALL 77
CLIFTON E. MARSH 78
DR. BOYCE WATKINS 79
ALABAMA STATE SENATOR HANK SANDERS 79
TUSKEGEE ALABAMA MAYOR JOHNNY FORD 81
NATIONAL REVIEW 82
FRANK PAUL JONES 82
PROF. ANDRE C. WILLIS 82
PRESIDENT IBRAHIM B. SYED, PH. D., ... 83
INTERNATIONAL ISLAMIC CONFERENCE 85
PROFESSOR MATTIAS GARDELL 86
SOCIALIST ECONOMIST AND PROFESSOR DR. MICHAEL D. YATES 87
HOLY PEOPLE OF THE WORLD: A CROSS-CULTURAL ENCYCLOPEDIA (MISBAHUDEEN AHMED RUFAI) 88
TIME MAGAZINE 89
PRESIDENT NELSON MANDELA 90
USA TODAY 90
JOURNALIST VINCE BEISER 92
JULIUS LESTER 93

TUSKEGEE-MACON COUNTY NAACP BRANCH 94

A PORTRAIT IN HUMILITY: WHAT DOES MINISTER FARRAKHAN THINK ABOUT HIMSELF? 99

HISTORICAL TIMELINE OF U.S. GOVERNMENT ATTACKS ON THE NATION OF ISLAM IN AMERICA 101

MINISTER FARRAKHAN VS. AMERICA'S TOUGHEST MINDS 103

MEASURING MINISTER FARRAKHAN'S ELECTRONIC IMPACT 108

THE BEST HELPER OF THE HONORABLE ELIJAH MUHAMMAD 111

A TIMELINE OF JEWISH ATTACKS AGAINST THE 115

NATION OF ISLAM AND MINISTER FARRAKHAN 115

MINISTER FARRAKHAN AS A DEFENDER OF BLACK PEOPLE 117

STONED FOR GOOD WORKS, PROPAGANDA KEEPS HIDDEN MINISTER FARRAKHAN'S STELLAR RECORD OF LEADERSHIP 119

THE CRUCIFIXION OF BLACK JESUS	124
FROM FARD TO FARRAKHAN: AMERICA'S PUNISHMENT OF MESSIANIC DISSIDENTS	135
10 REASONS TO SUPPORT MINISTER FARRAKHAN'S PRESENCE ON COLLEGE CAMPUSES	141
IS HELP FOR BLACKS, HURT FOR JEWS?	146
DID MINISTER LOUIS FARRAKHAN GIVE BIRTH TO HIP-HOP?	151
GOD GIVES THE MINISTER A VISION OF THINGS TO COME	155
FARRAKHAN PLAYS MENDELSSOHN	163
FARRAKHAN IS NOT THE PROBLEM: THE ARROGANCE AND ABSURDITY OF AMERICA'S RACIAL LITMUS TEST	169
PROFESSOR DERRICK BELL'S ANALYSIS OF MINISTER FARRAKHAN'S "RACIAL STANDING"	176
FARRAKHAN IS INNOCENT, FBI IS GUILTY	183
FARRAKHAN VINDICATED!	187
MIRACLE MAN OF THE MUSLIMS	194
IS FARRAKHAN THE NEW GARVEY?	203
BIBLIOGRAPHY	209
SPECIAL THANKS	216

Foreword

Brother Demetric Muhammad through the written word and visual presentation has provided us with powerful insight into the impact of the words, work, sacrifice and humility of the Honorable Minister Louis Farrakhan. His skillful weaving together of the recorded testimony of those who have openly opposed Minister Farrakhan and the Nation of Islam as well as others who admire and love him is one of the finest defenses of Truth anyone could develop. For those who only know Minister Farrakhan through second-hand sources, sound-bites, propaganda and half-truths, *Who Do They Say I Am: The Vindication of Minister Louis Farrakhan* not only clears up misinformation, it also provides a path directly into the *heart* of a human being who has touched every walk of life.

The Most Honored Elijah Muhammad wrote that the religious class and those most educated and accomplished in this world would be most opposed to his work of the resurrection of Black and oppressed people in America, the Western Hemisphere and all over the world, *yet* a critical mass of these *same* persons would eventually be persuaded by His Message and provide some of the greatest help possible to further and establish it during an especially dark hour.

As this prediction becomes manifestly true it is important that we understand the evolution of the conflicted thinking of such persons - initially blinded out of ignorance and genuine misunderstanding or envy, jealousy and vanity – but who are now able to see Minister Farrakhan more and more as Allah (God) and His Christ do; an essential man standing as both bridge and door between two worlds. As more and more of the brightest 'stars' of this world look up to Minister Farrakhan it paves the way for those who follow them to do the same. *Who Do They Say I Am: The Vindication of Minister Louis Farrakhan* uniquely chronicles and displays aspects of the hidden and secret thinking at work in all of us who wrestle with finding a balance between our hopes and fears and the consequences of our choices on ourselves, our families, our professional lives and our status in society. Many of us it seems, could and would accept Minister Farrakhan, if only we could overcome our fear of loss.

Allah (God) says in the Holy Qur'an, **"Never did We send a Warner to a population but the wealthy ones among them said: 'We believe not in the (Message) with which ye have been sent.'"** Certainly it is those who have been blessed with the wealth of finance; the wealth of knowledge; and the wealth of ability who are often slowest to respond to the message of truth. But when they finally do - their belief, hard work and pursuit of righteousness provides one of the most powerful forms of witness on behalf of both the Message and the Messenger. This wonderful book is but a snapshot of this phenomenon as well as the confluence of forces which produce it.

As one who has picked up his cross, as a disciple of Christ, Minister Farrakhan in lifting up His Teacher, has unintentionally moved to the core of a magnetic process, as it reads in the Book of John, "And I, if I be lifted up from the earth, will draw all men unto me." In compiling *Who Do They Say I Am: The Vindication of Minister Louis Farrakhan* Student Minister Demetric Muhammad is assisting in this process, described in I Peter 3:15, "...Always be prepared to give an answer to everyone who asks you to give the reason for the hope that you have. But do this with gentleness and respect." His approach not only brings to clear view the fire and courage of Minister Farrakhan in defending the truth but also the gentleness and respect which characterizes his treatment of people, regardless of their creed, class and color. And understanding *both* the words and character of Minister Farrakhan are an essential part of God's merciful plan of salvation, which requires courage and patient perseverance through much suffering.

The Honorable Elijah Muhammad taught that the worst famine in history was coming to America. As his National Representative, Minister Farrakhan has been the foremost instrument of God in the extension of this Warning.

In the 105th Psalms it reads, "*He called down famine on the land and destroyed all their supplies of food; and he sent a man before them— Joseph, sold as a slave. They bruised his feet with shackles, his neck was put in irons, till what he foretold came to pass, till the word of the LORD proved him true. The king sent and released him, the ruler of peoples set him free. He made him master of his household, ruler over all he possessed, to instruct his princes as he pleased and teach his elders wisdom.*" This book of witness - *Who Do They Say I Am: The Vindication of Minister Louis Farrakhan* - represents overwhelming evidence of this work in progress – the spiritual ascent and elevation of Minister Farrakhan in the minds of *both* the classes and the masses - in fulfillment of one of the most important prophecies in all of divine scripture.

Allah (God) says in the Holy Qur'an in part, "**Ye have indeed in the Messenger of Allah a beautiful pattern (of conduct) for any one whose hope is in Allah and the Final Day, and who engages much in the Praise of Allah.**" In Part 28 of his 'The Time and What Must Be Done' series, Minister Farrakhan revealed that when he was last in the Holy City of Medina - at the Mosque and Tomb of Prophet Muhammad (Peace Be Upon Him) - he uttered a prayer to Allah (God) that he be given a *double* portion of the spirit of Muhammad.

The moving testimony contained within *Who Do They Say I Am: The Vindication of Minister Louis Farrakhan* indicates that the Lord of The Worlds both heard and answered the prayer of this Servant of God.

There can only be a Divine explanation for what you are about to read.-

Brother Cedric Muhammad
July 31, 2013

Brother Cedric Muhammad is an economist and economic advisor to the African Union. He is a member of the Nation of Islam Research Group and founder of Blackelectorate.com and AfricaPreBrief.com. He is the author of the excellent 3 volume series of books entitled The Entrepreneurial Secret.

Preface

Allah (God) bears witness to his Messenger

"When the hypocrites come to thee, they say: We bear witness that thou art indeed Allah's messenger. ***And Allah knows thou art indeed His Messenger.*** *And Allah bears witness that the hypocrites are surely liars. (Al-Munafiqun: The Hypocrites. Chapter 63, verse 1)"*

It is a great honor, a humbling experience and profound privilege to be asked by the author, my Brother Demetric Muhammad, to offer my testimony in support of his new scholarship, *"Who Do They Say I Am?: The Vindication of Minister Louis Farrakhan."*

CONTEXT

This statement "Who do they say I am?" arises in the **context** of Jesus talking with his disciples as they were traveling to different areas in Palestine where Jesus performed his many miracles. *(Matthew 16:13-20 KJV).* It also is the basis for Peter's confession that Jesus is the Christ.

His disciples' answers to the question were varied. But the question is, "Why did Jesus have to ask his disciples who do they, the people, say I am?" Jesus performed many miracles; cleansing the leper, healing the woman with the issue of blood, and raising Lazarus from the dead. He would often tell those that he healed to not speak of it. Why? What did Jesus know about the talk that was circulating about him, that he wanted see if his disciples were aware. He also wanted to know how they saw him.

Many of the Jewish sects of that day, the scribes and Pharisees were attempting to trap Jesus into saying something that would violate Roman law, and thus cause him to be brought up on false charges. , especially the charge of sedition which was ultimately leveled against him. Jesus hearing them and knowing their thoughts would never be trapped by their skillful and deceptive questions. So, his enemies began circulating among the people to create a false reputation of Jesus and his good works. The Bible speaks of this in the Book of Revelations as the Serpent casting out of his mouth water as a flood after the woman (the Messenger of God), that he might cause her to be carried away of the flood. *(Rev. 12:15 KJV)*

When Jesus was falsely charged with sedition, speaking and acting against the authority of Rome, and mockingly charged with saying that he was the "king of the Jews" none of his disciples came forward to defend him. In fact the disciples denied him before the courts of Pontius Pilate.

The wicked frame mischief by means of the law. It is always the tactic, strategy and method of the wicked to create false charges. To use the law falsely against the prophets and Messengers of God. Because the wicked fear the people, who have a view of the Messenger as a man of great character and reputation, the wicked must first destroy the character and good reputation of the Messenger of God in the minds of the people.

This is so, that when they bring the Messenger of God before their courts with their false charges, the people will believe the false charges to be true and not rise up to oppose the unrighteous acts of the wicked and their government.

These events and circumstances of the past, in the time of Jesus, are unfolding today in our time, regarding the modern scribes and Pharisees and the modern example of Jesus today in the person of the Hon. Minister Louis Farrakhan. If we carefully studied scriptural history that we have shared a portion of in this writing, and overlay the facts and circumstances of yesterday with today, you will clearly see the same pattern. This is why such a book is necessary, because today the disciples should not deny the good character and reputation of a man who has given us all spiritual life. We must come forward to defend God's anointed servant, as it is our salvation to do so. Jesus was silent in the face of his accusers, because the trial was not really his, the trial was ours.

This book is purposed to present an answer to the question, who do the people say that Farrakhan is? Since at least 1984, the Hon. Minister Louis Farrakhan has been falsely charged by the modern scribes and Pharisees, the Synagogue of Satan, with being mad, anti-Semitic, anti-white, homophobic, and a hater. Nothing could be further from the Truth.

The wicked have spewed their negative flood of propaganda against the Hon.

Minister Louis Farrakhan for the last 29 years through the mass media of publications and broadcasting that they have an inordinate ownership and control over. This book will help the earth (the people) to open their mouths, and swallow the flood, the negative and false propaganda of the synagogue of Satan against the anointed servant of Allah (God), the Hon. Minister Louis Farrakhan. *(Rev. 12:16 KJV)*. The aim of these wicked acts on the part of the Synagogue of Satan are to destroy the good name, good character, and good reputation of the Hon. Minister Louis Farrakhan in the minds of the people. This is so, when they use their courts of law to bring false charges against the Hon. Minister Louis Farrakhan and the Nation of Islam, their hope is that there will be no outcry against this wickedness by the people whom they fear.

CHARACTER AND REPUTATION

What is character and what is reputation? Character is defined as *the aggregate of features and traits that form the individual nature of some person or thing, moral or ethical quality, qualities of honesty, courage, or the like; integrity*. This definition perfectly fits the character of the Hon. Minister Louis Farrakhan. The Holy Quran defends the character of the Messenger by stating that the Messenger has sublime morals. *(Al-Qalam: The Pen: Chapter 68, verse 4)*.

My venerable evidence professor and dean from law school taught us that in a court of law, especially in the criminal context, character evidence is really not evidence of a person's character at all. Character is an intrinsic trait, such that only God, and maybe the person, actually knows the character of the self.

He taught us that it is actually testimony about the reputation of the person that is offered to give an indication of what the character of the individual may be.

Reputation is defined as the *estimation in which a person or thing is held, especially by the community or the public generally*. Thus, the Synagogue of Satan works in this area to slander and defame the good name and reputation of the Messenger of God in the minds of people. This they have attempted to accomplish against the Honorable Minister Louis Farrakhan up to the very minute of the writing of this testimony.

They have not been successful, and they will not be successful. As the Holy

Qur'an teaches, the Messenger of Allah (God) is an excellent example for any believer who hopes in Allah and the latter day, and remembers Allah much. *(Al-Ahzab: The Allies: Chapter 33 verse 21).*

The reputation of the Hon. Minister Louis Farrakhan is as different as the night is from the day, and as far away as the Sun is from the planet Pluto, depending upon who you talk with. Among the people whom he is anointed to serve, which is black people, and all oppressed people and humanity itself, he is seen as a man of truth, a lover of humanity, one who speaks truth to power, and hates the wicked actions not only of Satan and his Synagogue, but also those of us who may individually engage in wicked practices, regardless to creed or class or color. He is first and foremost a lover of Almighty God and His Truth, and the Mission of His Messenger Messiah. He loves his people, which he has demonstrated by sacrificing his life to see human beings made better. The Bible teaches us that no greater love than this, that a man would lay down his life for his friends. *(John 15:13).* The Minister has proved this to see us free, justified and equal, and to return humanity back to the oneness of Allah (God).

He proves among us each day the bible's teachings, that you should love god with all your heart, soul, mind and strength and love your neighbor as yourself. These are the two great commandments given by Jesus to his disciples. *(Matt. 22:37-40)*

THE REBUILDING

It is necessary that we retrace our footsteps, and review the demonstration of the good character and reputation of the Hon. Minister Louis Farrakhan, as well as some of the attacks of the wicked. In hopes that we will not continue to make mistakes in our understanding and view of Allah (God's) blessing to us by his presence among us. The Most Honorable Elijah Muhammad said that History is best qualified to reward our research. It develops the springs and motives of Human Conduct. If our conduct and behavior is to be rightly guided, then the scripture teaches us "how can they know, except they have a teacher, and how can they have a teacher except he be sent" *(Rom. 10:14-15)*

During the first or second week of September 1977, the scales fell from the Hon. Minister Louis Farrakhan's eyes, and he accepted the assignment to rebuild the work of the Hon. Elijah Muhammad, as scripture prophesied he would.

Jesus had prayed for Peter, that his faith would not fail him altogether, and when he returned to Christ, then he should go and strengthen his brethren. (Luke 22:31-32).

The Hon. Elijah Muhammad promised the Minister that *"there will be two backing you up Brother, Allah and Myself."* The journey that led to this event in September of 1977 involves Bro. Akbar Muhammad and Bro. Jabril Muhammad, among others. Both men have magnificent testimonies on these events. I have heard the Hon. Minister Louis Farrakhan relate some of these events, however the beauty and magnificence of Allah (God) working in and through his anointed servant, requires an exactness of recitation that will require further research and exploration. Of course the Hon. Minister Louis Farrakhan is best at explaining the actual facts of those events

For seven years the Hon. Minister Louis Farrakhan traveled throughout America, and especially among the youth on college campuses to reestablish the teachings of the Hon. Elijah Muhammad. In 1979 I became one of those college students that he met and taught as I went to see him at Coppin State teachers college in Baltimore Maryland.

The Minister would not do interviews with the media. He shared with me that the Hon. Elijah Muhammad taught him that when a seed is germinating in the earth, that it sends its roots down deep into the earth, long before it sends a reed up through the earth. And even though the reed may look weak, it is firmly rooted in the earth. The Hon. Minister Louis Farrakhan worked quietly like this building study groups among college students and in individuals homes. There would be several study groups studying the teachings of the Hon. Elijah Muhammad in the same city and they would not know the existence of each other. This led to our first Saviours' Day in the Rebirth of the Nation of Islam.

Although it is commonly believed that the Most Honorable Elijah Muhammad is physically dead, The Honorable Minister Louis Farrakhan declared in his first Saviours' Day Message in the rebuilding of the Nation of

Islam on February 22, 1981 at the Auditorium Theater in Chicago before thousands of persons, that the Honorable Elijah Muhammad was physically alive, and that He had escaped a death plot, and was with His Sender Master Fard Muhammad on the Wheel. A giant mechanical object that the Honorable Elijah Muhammad said fulfilled Ezekiel's vision of a wheel within a wheel. *(Ezekiel1:1-28)*

The Honorable Minister Louis Farrakhan though vilified, maligned, and evil spoken of, even by his own people, for his assertion that he believed that the Honorable Elijah Muhammad was in fact alive, traveled the Country on a 43 city speaking tour, teaching on the spiritual subjects "The Time and What Must be Done" and "In Christ, All Things Are Possible".

In 1983 the Honorable Minister Louis went on another speaking tour entitled, 'Christ's Imminent Return: He Makes All Things New". Many of these teaching were at Christian Churches, which surprised many Christians who assumed that Muslims did not believe in Jesus Christ. In 1984, The Honorable Minister Louis Farrakhan announced his support for the Presidential Candidacy of the Reverend Jesse L. Jackson, Sr. When Rev. Jesse Jackson embraced Yassir Arafat and the struggle of the Palestinian people, he began to receive death threats from some Jewish groups.

When the Minister warned certain members of the Jewish community about the consequences of their death threats against the life of Reverend Jackson, he was called a Black Hitler. When he defended himself against such false charges, the wicked scribes (which are the writers and broadcasters of the press) falsely accused the Minister of praising Hitler and later also falsely accused the Minister of calling Judaism a "gutter religion". In 1985, after his address at the Forum in Los Angeles before 19,000 people, the cry among the members of the Jewish community was that they wanted The Honorable Minister Louis Farrakhan dead.

MORE THAN A VISION
It was in this murderous climate that after his speech he left Los Angeles and went into Mexico, and there he and his wife Mother Khadijah were in a hotel in Tepoztlan, where he had on many occasions climbed the mountain and visited a temple built on top of that mountain in honor of Quetzalcoatl the

Christ figure of Mezzo America or Central America. On the night of September 17th 1985 he had a *"more than a vision experience,"* and in that experience he was transported to the Wheel by a little baby plane that singled him out from among a group of persons, and took him to the Mother Wheel where he was ushered into a room. He saw a scroll roll down in front of him with cursive writing and when he went to read the writing it disappeared and then he heard the voice of his Teacher, the Most Honorable Elijah Muhammad telling him of plans made by the President and his joint Chiefs of Staff in early September 1985, that the President (Reagan) had planned a war. The Minister was never told where the war would be, or who it would be against, but he was told in that communication to hold a Press Conference and make the President's plan known. The Hon. Elijah Muhammad instructed the Minister as follows; *"and tell them, you got it from me, Elijah Muhammad on the Wheel."* The Minister was then told by the Hon. Elijah Muhammad, that he had one more thing to do, and when that was completed, he could come again to the Wheel where he would be allowed to see him face to face.

When the Minister awakened he did not remember this experience and it wasn't until an earthquake hit Mexico City on September 19th that affected Tepoztlan that his experience on the night of September 17th came back to him and he shared it for the first time with his wife Mother Khadijah and Mother Tynetta Muhammad, the wife of the Honorable Elijah Muhammad.

Fresh from that experience, the Minister went to New York City to hold our first Saviours' Day in honor of the birth of the Most Honorable Elijah Muhammad, on October 7, 1985, where 50,000 people tried to get into Madison Square Garden to hear the Honorable Minister Louis Farrakhan. Every seat was taken and even the aisles had people in them and the adjunct building the Felt Forum was filled, and 20,000 more people were in the streets trying to get in to hear the message. Once again the climate of hate created by the Anti-Defamation League (ADL), and the Jewish Defense League (JDL) and the press, incited protesters from the Jewish Defense League who were chanting in frenzy, "Who do you want?" Farrakhan! "How Do You Want Him? Dead!

In December 1985 the Minister started his first World Friendship Tour in the Virgin Islands, he went to Jamaica, Barbados and from Barbados to Panama where he was rejected in several hotels, due to Jewish pressure. He was banned from traveling to Bermuda, the island where his mother grew up and where his grandmother and grandfather are buried. That ban was subsequently lifted by the work of Minister Byron Muhammad known as Hamid Abdullah. The Minister was also banned from the United Kingdom (England) and that ban still exists today.

In Panama Brother Minister Akbar Muhammad, our International Representative had made reservations at the Marriott Hotel and they were rejected; they were rejected at a second hotel, and at a third hotel reservations were made under an alias, but when the Hotel found out that it was the Minister and his delegation, they were asked to leave but refused. This happened because of the hatred that was falsely projected against him by the Synagogue of Satan, which had been spread throughout the world.

The Honorable Minister Louis Farrakhan went on to speak in Panama in Colon and from there he went to Honduras, and while he was in Belize City, President Ronald Reagan came on television and issued an executive order that stopped all Americans from traveling to and doing business with Libya. The Executive Order also directed that any American traveling to Libya would be fined and sentenced up to 10 years in federal prison.

The Honorable Minister Louis Farrakhan then came back to the United States to prepare for the second leg of the journey and in early February 1986 he was visited by Kwame Ture (formerly known as Stokely Carmichael) and he asked the Minister if he would hold a Press Conference at the National Press Club in Washington D.C. where there were 15 groups that would stand with him to say *"hands off Libya."* The Minister agreed and flew to Washington and wrote the speech that he would give at the National Press Club which was approved by Kwame Ture and four other groups that were willing to stand with The Minister during that time in delivering this speech. At the press conference as the Minister saw all of the camera's bright lights flashing in the back of the room, it reminded him of his experience. And it crystalized for him that the war was against Libya and its Leader Muammar Gadhafi.

Notwithstanding the Executive order banning travel to Libya, the Hon. Minister Louis Farrakhan showing his character and courage, went to Libya, and based upon his *"more than a vision experience"* shared his belief that President Reagan planned attack Libya. This saved the life of President Muammar Gadhafi, when President Reagan bombed Libya in 1986. The Attorney General of the United States, Edwin Meese in a news article, threatened to arrest the Minister on his return to the United States. A law firm hired by the Nation under the direction of Attorney Ava Muhammad filed a lawsuit against President Reagan and his Secretary of State George Schultz, and Attorney General Edwin Meese. The government backed away from their claim to arrest the Minister and the court dismissed the case.

Also during this period in the late 1980's President Reagan, as a staunch anti-communist, felt that Nicaragua could not fall to a socialist regime, and since Congress had not allocated any of the tax payer's money, to fund opposition against a socialist regime coming to power, he went around Congress to fight the war. Saudi Arabia gave financial assistance to the Reagan Administration to fund a War against the Contras. It was also during the Reagan administration, that a counter Whitehouse was set up in the basement by Col. Oliver North to sell drugs among black people in the Ghettos of America to fund the War in Nicaragua.

During this time in History, tens of thousands were flocking to hear the message of the Honorable Minister Louis Farrakhan. Why was this War waged by an American Administration in Nicaragua significant? It is because every time there is a major rising of the consciousness in the Black Community, it is followed by the introduction of drugs into the community. The money generated from this government run drug trafficking enterprise in the Black Community was used to fund the War in Nicaragua. In the 1960's there was Heroin introduced into the black community as a response to the rise of Consciousness and militancy among Black people. This was primarily due to the teachings of the Hon. Elijah Muhammad and his principal student Malcolm X. In the 1980's there was crack cocaine. This was the beginning of the crack cocaine epidemic that swept the West Coast through our unknowing Brother "Freeway" Rick Ross. And just as opium was used to drug the Chinese and bring silver out of China, the same strategy has been used here to rob the Black community of 400 billion dollars generated by our Black economy by bringing crack in the U.S. and taking money out of the Black community to finance a war in Central America. This epidemic swept through the Ghettos of America like a cancer, and we saw the emergence of the "New Jack City" era.

From 1984 on the Minister was under vicious assault by some in the Jewish community who were bitterly angry with Him for his defense of the Reverend Jesse Jackson. He was referred to by them as a "Black Hitler," which made members of the Jewish community afraid, and of the mind that a new Hitler had to be dealt with before he became powerful.

It is also interesting that the 17th Chapter of the Holy Qur'an is called the Israelites and on the night of the 17th of September the Honorable Minister Louis Farrakhan had his experience, and in this Chapter of the Holy Qur'an it opens referring to the night vision of Prophet Muhammad.

The Minister came to understand that the war planned by the President had two aspects; a Muslim leader and county in the East, but also on this side in America a Muslim Leader with Black American youth. With gang warfare spreading, you had the Crips and the Bloods, and Minister Farrakhan immediately went on tour speaking to Black people about Stop the Killing. After this tour the Minister began the Men's only Meetings.

He was told by a Nigerian, do not do that because the government might think that you are trying to raise an army and this will bring the wrath of the government down upon you. He listened but also remembering the experience on the wheel, he went into major cities speaking to tens and hundreds of thousands of Black men and that inspired the Million Man March.

As the night vision of Prophet Muhammad created division among Muslims. They wanted to know, did he go in reality or was it a vision? This set a division among the Muslims, because it might make people think the Prophet was crazy, silly or mad. So it is with the Hon. Minister Louis Farrakhan's *"more than a vision experience."* There are mixed feelings and controversy around the subject. The Holy Qur'an vindicates the Messenger of God against the false charge that he is mad, and assures him that his reward will never be cut off by the wicked. *(Al-Qalam: The Pen Chapter 86 verses 1-6)*

In 1989 the Hon. Minister Louis Farrakhan held a press conference at the Marriott, Hotel in Washington D.C. In following the instructions of the Hon. Elijah Muhammad he made the announcement concerning his experience. The Minister warned the Government of America *"that before you can make mockery of me you will see these things [wheels] over major cities."* That night in Washington Fifteen Squadrons of 4 of these Wheels were seen in Washington over the U. S. Capitol and White House, proving the power of Allah (God) that was backing his servant, the Honorable Minister Louis Farrakhan. The Minister was also accompanied by the wheels after his speech in New York.

Every succeeding President has had an altercation with the Muslim World. In his experience the Minister was never given a name, he was told, "the President" and each President has planned some aspect of war with the Muslim World, but the biggest of all at that time was President George W. Bush.

DIVINE WARNER
On May 3rd, 2004, the Honorable Minister Louis Farrakhan, held a press conference at the National Press Club in Washington D.C. entitled "Guidance in A Time of Trouble: To America and the World." At this press conference the Honorable Minister Louis Farrakhan shared with the World, the guidance he shared with President Bush, based on his experience.

What the Honorable Minister Louis Farrakhan told President George W. Bush in his letters of December 1, 2001 and October 30, 2002, is the consequences he would face, if he carried out what Allah (God) had revealed to him was in the mind of President Bush about going to War in Iraq. President Bush did not heed the guidance and ran right into those consequences, and it destroyed his presidency, as he left being considered the worst President in U.S. History.

The Minister has come to understand more deeply the meaning of his *"more than a vision experience."* The experience is such a part of his DNA that every time he has spoken of his experience, he has told it the exact same way. This bears witness to the reality of his experience. It started in the second term of President Ronald Reagan, who has passed away, and his bombing of Libya. From the Minister's *"more than a vision experience"* we have had five Presidents. Mr. Reagan for 8 years, George H. W. Bush for 4 years, William Jefferson Clinton for 8 years, George W. Bush for 8 years, and now President Barack Obama for 5 years. It has been 28 years since The Honorable Minister Louis Farrakhan received this revelation, and the things that he has been able to see from the communication and from the experience that he had on the wheel with the Hon. Elijah Muhammad, is what has led to the Stop the Killing Tours, the Men only Meetings, and ultimately the Million Man March in 1995, the Million Family March in 2000 and the Millions More Movement in 2005. He saw a war being planned against Black youth, especially the black male in the United States. In 2012 he has led the FOI and MGT back into the streets to save our people from the evil of the genocidal plans against them.

This writer believes that we may be reaching the fulfillment of the meaning of the experience of the Hon. Minister Louis Farrakhan during the Presidency of Barack Obama, and in the revealing of the Synagogue of Satan in the yearlong broadcasts of "The Time and What Must Be Done". The Minister attempted to give guidance to President Obama on his actions in Libya at a press conference on March 31, 2011 at Mosque Maryam. He also warned the U.N. in a press conference on June 15, 2011 at the UN Plaza Hotel about NATO's aggression against the people of Libya based upon the wicked propaganda from our government. Such advice went unheeded which resulted in the death of President Muammar Gadhafi, and the American Ambassador to Libya.

This is some of the record of good works of the Hon. Minister Louis Farrakhan. We must remember, defend and uphold his good character, reputation and morals. Allah (God) has already promised us the victory. Let us always be ready to defend him and the truth that he represents. As the Holy Qur'an tells us of the Hon. Minister Louis Farrakhan in the 53rd Chapter, called *Al-Najm-The Star*.

"In the name of Allah, the Beneficent, the Merciful. By the Star when it sets! Your companion errs not, nor does he deviate. Nor does he speak out of desire. It is naught but revelation that is revealed. One Mighty in Power has taught him. The Lord of Strength. So he attained to perfection. And he is in the highest part of the horizon. Then he drew near, drew nearer yet, So he was the measure of two bows or closer still. So He revealed to His servant what He revealed. The heart was not untrue in seeing what he saw." (Al-Najm: The Star Chapter 53 verses 1-11)

Let us not be untrue to what we see of a man of good character, reputation and morals. He is already vindicated with Allah (God). We should take Allah's coloring.

Abdul Arif Muhammad
August 12, 2013

Abdul Arif Muhammad is a helper of the Hon. Minister Louis Farrakhan, a Student in the Ministry, an attorney, historian, researcher, writer, lecturer and former Editor-in-Chief of The Final Call newspaper. He also serves as General Counsel of the Nation of Islam and is a member of the Nation of Islam Research Group

Introduction

Mixed Feelings and Controversy

Examining The Pattern of Reaction To The Ministry of The Honorable Minister Louis Farrakhan As The Struggle Against Prophetic and Revolutionary Magnetism

In the name of Allah, the Beneficent, the Merciful.

(By) the inkstand and the pen and that which they write! By the grace of thy Lord thou art not mad. And surely thine is a reward never to be cut off. And surely thou hast sublime morals. So thou wilt see, and they (too) will see, Which of you is mad. Surely thy Lord knows best who is erring from His way, and He knows best those who go aright. So obey not the rejecters. They wish that thou shouldst be pliant, so they (too) would be pliant. And obey not any mean swearer, Defamer, going about with slander, Hinderer of good, outstepping the limits, sinful, Ignoble, besides all that, notoriously mischievous Surah 68:1-13

It has been such a great joy for me to research, study and reflect over the tremendous life and work of the Honorable Minister Louis Farrakhan during the production of this book. This book began as part of an assignment that I received while serving as a member of Minister Farrakhan's research team. The assignment involved preparing research material that would educate and prepare a small team of Muslim marketing professionals, who would work together to help promote the wide spread distribution of the Honorable Minister Louis Farrakhan's message using modern marketing tools. What I discovered in the process of carrying out that assignment is that there had not been any serious examination of the Minister's impact on groups and persons outside of the Nation of Islam.

At the root of this lack of research emphasis is that The Minister for more than 36 years has been the target of hate filled slander and strategic propaganda coming from various Jewish groups who have an economic interest in opposing the Self-Help message of Minister Farrakhan. Their propaganda and slander against Minister Farrakhan has produced something of a veritable prison of public opinion that the Minister is inside of. And those of us who love The Minister continue to write, educate, inform and otherwise seek to influence public opinion with our own fact-filled counter-narrative to what is widely distributed through the major media sources on behalf of groups who are anti-Farrakhan. But as a member of the Nation of Islam under Minister Farrakhan's direct leadership, it is rather an expected response that I and others would extol the Minister's many virtues and noble character. What is not necessarily expected is those outside of the Nation of Islam's membership expressing love, admiration and respect for such a much maligned man-the man who is affectionately known as "The Minister."

So this book begins with a profound compilation of quotes from an eclectic and diverse group that includes elected officials, celebrities, religious leaders, professors, and journalists whose words and expressions about Minister Farrakhan are not what one might expect, especially if you have only known of The Minister through sound bites and the routinely doctored snippets taken from hours long lectures. This compilation is a very substantial amount of praise, admiration, gratitude, respect and love. It is of such quantity, it causes one to see it as very "weighty" evidence in support of The Minister who is frequently tried in the court of public opinion. These quotes therefore are real testimonies from what we can consider The Minister's character witnesses. This kind of testimony and "witness bearing" is very important. It is so important because it foils the various efforts at the character assassination of The Minister.

The history of both Prophets and Revolutionaries is replete with the recorded attempts of their enemies to assassinate their character. When the corrupt rulers and religious leaders, who are the frequent object of the prophet's and revolutionary's protest and condemnation, can assassinate their character, they then carry out their planned physical assassination with ease. Their muddying the reputation and good name of the Prophets and Revolutionaries ensures that the masses of the people will neither protest nor rise to defend the Prophets and Revolutionaries during the hour of their persecution.

As you read these statements and observations, it will become easy to see that Minister Louis Farrakhan is the inheritor of the legacy, tradition, spirit, mind and will of the scripture's Prophets and history's revolutionaries. He is therefore epitomized in this way; he is unique and special in this way. And in my opinion, Minister Farrakhan's impact, value and character cannot be fully and accurately determined without due consideration of how he, in the most critical of time periods, embodies prophets and revolutionaries. This is critical because Minister Farrakhan represents how the perfect harmony or balance between the sacred and the secular is achieved. What I mean by this is that there are certain human beings who exist as the embodiment of what other human beings who lived long before them desired and expected. These kinds of human beings we could say are born with a pre-determined idea; some would consider them to be "seeds of yearning." The Prophets of religion have often been such persons. The Scientists and Inventors have been such persons. The political Revolutionaries and social reformers have been such persons.

These special individuals fulfill and answer certain problems that existed before them. They fill gaps and voids. Such individuals contain in them what history wanted, what the present needs and what the future will comprised of. They are exemplars, emblems and models.

This aspect of who and what Minister Farrakhan is explains how he is more than a Black leader, great orator and activist religious leader. This aspect of who and what Minister Farrakhan is, also explains why he is more than a prophet or messenger from God and more than a political Revolutionary. He is unique. Perhaps the best historical figure to provide similitude to who and what the Minister Farrakhan is, is the Jesus of the Gospels, who was, according to scholars, both prophet and revolutionary. And like Jesus, Minister Farrakhan proves that the root of the religious prophet and secular (non-religious) revolutionary is the same frustration, exasperation and pain over the present condition of the world and its people--the same ancient universal yearning for balance, perfection and completion. So in Minister Farrakhan we see Jesus, but we also see Nat Turner; we see Muhammad but we also see Martin Luther; we see Aaron, Elisha and Paul, but we also see Garvey, MLK and Brother Malcolm. His leadership therefore eliminates the false choice of "either or;" his is a synthesis that provides for our people "and both," on the question of the secular or the sacred path toward liberation.

In his voice is a characteristic musical and harmonious delivery of mighty truths and profound wisdom. But his messages are not just musical in cadence, tone and effect; the content of his messages harmonize and synthesize the best wisdom of all leaders, sages, prophets, and revolutionaries who lived before him. This aspect of his role and his ability is in similitude to the book of scripture of the Muslims called the Holy Qur'an. For in the Qur'an is essential truths that have been by Allah (God) revealed so that the Qur'an as the last of the revelatory books, would itself be a harmonious synthesis of the best wisdom and teachings of all scriptures that were revealed before it. And what one hears in the epic and august messages of Minister Farrakhan of the voices and strategies of the best of history's heroes.

So, much of what these "witnesses" have declared regarding The Minister is borne of their examining the very curious phenomenon that The Minister has become. They have examined him through the lens of their profession, their educational background, their race, their political orientation and their hopes and expectations. Their examination of Minister Farrakhan that we have compiled here deserves great study. In the study of the natural world, the field of Chemistry emphasized the study of "reactions." This is of note because human interactions are often described as having "Chemistry" or not having "Chemistry." An old Arab proverb suggests that reactions are of special merit in determining the relative strength or importance of a man. That proverb states that "you don't judge a man by who his friends are, but by who his enemies are." In fact, often are prominent Black people polled and examined to determine if and to what degree they have been affected by what could be termed as the "Farrakhan reagent" that is present in the atmosphere. This occurrence is often referred to as "The Farrakhan Litmus Test." Litmus tests are used in chemical reactions and are defined as being *a coloring material (obtained from lichens) that turns red in acid solutions and blue in alkaline solutions; used as a very rough acid-base indicator.* The idea of The Farrakhan Litmus Test is therefore to identify to what degree has Minister Farrakhan's message and ideas saturated the hearts and minds of the Blacks who occupy prominent positions within American society. It is to determine if such persons have become "acidic" or consciously averse to the reigning idea of "white supremacy" that has ill-effected every institution and every sphere of public and professional life. And all who fail The Farrakhan Litmus Test are forced to pay a price. Many endure and suffer great loss as a result of possessing a favorable opinion of The Honorable Minister Louis Farrakhan. This is a reality that must come to an end!

At this point in my continuing study of what these courageous "witnesses" have provided for us in the way of defending the character and reputation of The Minister, I find a very interesting trend of reactions. It might be considered something of a "moth to a flame" reaction.

Like a moth to a flame, the elite, the mighty, the wealthy and the famous are frequently attracted to the phenomenal presence of the Honorable Minister Louis Farrakhan. Consider the flame for a moment. The source of the flame's attractive power is its warmth, color, light, movement and energy. The flame then, has aesthetics, substance, purpose and a beneficial function. As the moth comes closer it risks becoming consumed by the flame that has so attracted it. In the case of these prominent persons who have examined The Minister, we find a certain excitement and enthusiasm with The Minister's ability to do things that others simply cannot do. Specifically, his ability to accurately identify problems in the Black community and address them in a way no one else can. They admire his ability to attract and draw crowds in the tens of thousands, even at what is considered in today's world, an advanced age. They marvel at how he can reform Black people who have previously been destroyed by the effects of institutional racism and what it produces of self-destructive life-styles. He is regularly cited for his oration and preaching ability that is exceptionally better than any who one would consider as his peers. Some have examined him from a close distance and comment on his humility, sincerity and great appetite for learning. Other are awe-struck over his beautiful appearance and courage to "speak truth to power," for he is the most beautiful of revolutionaries.

Invariably however, these human "moths" feel the need to stay at a safe distance so as not to become fully consumed with The Minister's message and its revolutionary ideas. We find this demonstrated when there are complimentary expressions regarding The Minister mixed with "complain-itory" expressions about The Minister. And this is quite intriguing. For it suggests that who The Minister is and what he says draws and pulls on his examiner on a deep level, but they often feel conflicted internally because what he says and does, that they are naturally drawn to and are affected by, does violence to the ideas and previously held beliefs that they hold on to in their minds. So they are drawn in to him because their heart is in agreement with him; but what is in their head is in opposition to him because their mind has been formed and fashioned by a whole host of life experiences in the hostile American environment where the philosophy of white supremacy and black inferiority continue to dominate the Black American zeitgeist.

So what follows is as much about Minister Farrakhan's great magnetism as it is about prominent and powerful persons wrestling with being magnetically drawn to a man that they are expected to loathe and hate. These mixed feelings surrounding the controversial presence of Minister Louis Farrakhan are similar, and in many instances identical, to the mixed feelings surrounding scripture's prophets.

The prophets were mocked by the "chiefs and leaders" of the people. They were called mad. The Arabic word *majnun* is translated as "mad" in the

English translation of the Holy Qur'an. The word *majnun* is from the root word *janna*, which is the same root as the word *jinn*. In Islamic cultures the jinn are believed to be hidden beings who oppose mankind whenever he strays from the path of righteous. The root word *janna* means "to be mad, dark, covered or hidden." This suggests that the prophet's alleged "madness" was coming from a hidden source or that there was much "more than what meets the eye." This is exactly the case where The Minister is concerned. His passion and bold forthright condemnation of racism and injustice do in fact emerge from a hidden source. But that hidden source is not evil or malicious.

Minister Farrakhan has been called anti-Semitic, anti-White, homophobic, anti-American and a teacher of hate. These are all the modern manifestations of the ancient scriptures foretelling and forth telling of the prophets of Allah (God) being labeled as "mad."

Allah (God) Himself is described in the Holy Qur'an as being hidden. In Arabic, Allah's (God's) hiddenness is denoted by the use of the Arabic word *ghaib*, which is oft-times loosely translated as "unseen." And it is the unseen or hidden Allah who raises from among troubled and deviant societies a man that he makes into a prophet (nabi and rasul). The English translation of the Holy Qur'an approximately 49 times refers to these prophets as *warners*.

These divine warners to corrupt and wayward governments and peoples bring good news of Allah's concern over the condition of the people; but they warn these societies that if they continue with the business of sin as usual, that Allah (God) will chastise them for their wicked practices. And since warnings seek to prevent the loss of life and property it is not done in a common ordinary tone. Warnings are delivered with a sense of urgency. Warnings are meant to be alarming. Warnings and warners are meant to offend. Therefore, a divine warner who has been commissioned by Allah (God) to warn a people whose evil outweighs their good has an alarming, unnerving and controversial presence. Consider the following verse of scripture from the Holy Qur'an:

Corruption has appeared in the land and the sea on account of that which men's hands have wrought, that He may make them taste a part of that which they have done, so that they may return. Surah 30:41

Prophets, messengers and divine warners historically have been a source of agitation to the ruling class and to the wealthy of corrupt nations. Even the Hebrew word for prophet, *naba*, is suggests the warner delivers his warning with passion, spontaneity and force. The Old Testament being translated into English from Hebrew translates the word *naba* as *prophet*. *Naba* means *"To prophesy, to bubble up, to gush forth, to pour forth or to chant"*.

So while the corrupt rulers of America, have painted a picture of Minister Farrakhan as a madman, it is Minister Farrakhan's similitude to the prophets of the scriptures that perfectly explains his function, behavior and the reaction of the people to him.

The testimonies that follow provide a powerful never before seen counter-narrative to the propaganda that has been used to keep The Minister in a prison of public opinion. These are the authentic, honest reactions to Minister Farrakhan's noble character, beneficial impact and indispensable value to Black people, to America and all of humanity.

It is my sincere prayer that what we offer in this volume will free Minister Farrakhan from being negatively thought of by the American people. We pray that college students will be free to invite him and his representatives to speak on their campuses. We pray that pastors and ministers will see the value in opening the doors of their houses of worship to Minister Farrakhan's ministry. We pray that the Islamic world will unite with The Minister in building a model Muslim ummah in America. We pray that Black professionals will seek ways to offer their expertise and skills to aid The Minister solve the problems of the Black masses.

It is late in the evening for America. Minister Louis Farrakhan is the last prophetic voice that America will receive. He is a manifestation of God's willingness to extend mercy to America in spite of her great and unmatched sins. I encourage to read, reflect, and act.

May Allah bless you and your family with the light of understanding

Brother Demetric Muhammad

8-14-2013

What Do They Say About Farrakhan?

Former Governor of Pennsylvania and Mayor of Philadelphia, Ed Rendell

"I would like to thank the Nation of Islam here in Philadelphia. To thank you for what you stand for and what you stand for all the good it does to so many people in Philadelphia. And if there is anybody out here…who doesn't know, this is a faith that has as its principles, the family. This is a faith that doesn't just talk about family values, it lives family values. This is a faith where men respect their women and children and they manifest that faith by staying in the home with them. This is a faith that doesn't just talk about being against drugs but is out there every single day and night fighting against drugs. This is a faith that just doesn't talk about the value of education, it imbues in their children and schools that education is the way to opportunity." (H. M. Farrakhan 1997)

Actor and Celebrity Bruce Willis

Like a character in one of his movies, Bruce Willis came out blazing with both barrels in a George magazine interview, calling Bob Dole a ``nitwit,'' pronouncing Louis Farrakhan ``a hero of mine'' and declaring that organized religions are ``dying forms.'' The ``Die Hard'' star told the political magazine edited by John F. Kennedy Jr. that if he were black, ``I'd be with Farrakhan, too.''

``A lot of people feel Louis Farrakhan stands for a lot of negative things,'' Willis said of the Nation of Islam leader. ``But he is raising his voice against inequality. Anyone who stands up against injustice is a hero of mine.'' Willis also said he switched from Democrat to Republican in 1992 and supported President Bush for re-election because he felt Bill Clinton's campaign was too divisive. But he sat out the 1996 election between Dole and President Clinton because he considered the Republican ``a nitwit.''

Willis also criticized organized religions, which he called ``dying forms.'' ``Modern religion is the end trail of modern mythology,'' he said. ``But there are people who interpret the Bible literally. Literally! I choose not to believe that's the way. And that's what makes America cool, you know?" (Associated Press 1998)

Rapper Chuck D

"Farrakhan scares people, at least white people. But a lot of people who attack him have never even heard the man. They just take quotes that the media throws out at them. Farrakhan is a man I believe in and a lot of black people believe in because he lays everything out logically." (Hilburn 1988)

Rapper Nas

FC: Now, of course, the song that's being talked about, the song "Louis Farrakhan." Take us into your thinking when you laid down the lyrics to that.

NAS: Louis Farrakhan has made me cry. You know, what do you say about that, you know what I'm saying? When you see a man who put his life on the line for something—be he right or wrong—you admire him. But to me, Farrakhan is all the way right! I'm not sitting here going line for line, detail for detail, everything he says and all of that. It's a whole body of work that he's laid—he's laid his life down for his people. No matter if you like it or not. Anybody like that I admire. And, you know, anybody in this position, they would kill off. He was smart enough to say "I have an army who believe in what I'm saying, that this is the Truth." That "I would die for everyone, every soldier in that army." They believe that and they know that's true. So, you know, how could I not acknowledge that's that; that's what I acknowledge in my life, then, it's going to bleed into the music. It's not even on purpose. It just happened. It's just my thoughts. "Some revolutionaries get old, although I'm told..." you know?

It's like everybody's scared to speak out about what's in their heart, just because they're scared of who is going to come down on them. They're scared they're going to get "blacklisted." They're going to get all their endorsements taken away from them. They're scared that they can't feed their families. I understand that, but I admire those people who know that, and still go and do what they have to do, you know what I mean? If I had enough money, I'd buy him a Rolls Royce tomorrow! You know what I'm saying? Like, that's just how I feel about him!

He is a serious piece of history, you know, coming from Elijah Muhammad; coming from Malcolm X, coming from—that part of history is so special because it's what America is scared to talk about. They're scared to talk about that. And, if they would talk about it, it would help a lot of people. I know a lot of White cats that listen to Farrakhan! I went to a Coldplay concert, and his introduction was Farrakhan's speech! So, I was blown away! I'm sitting next to Gwyneth Paltrow—we're rocking to a Farrakhan speech! So, it made me go: "Damn! If he—why didn't I use that in my music? I've been wanting to!" So I'm just trying to show the love back now. (A. Muhammad, Hip Hop Lives: FCN Interview with Nas 2008)

5 term Memphis Mayor Willie Herenton

Among the Memphis notables present during the events held by the Nation of Islam were County Commissioners Sidney Chism and Henri Brooks, State Rep. G.A. Hardaway, state Sen. Reginald Tate and City Councilman Joe Brown. On Sunday, Mayor Pro Tem Myron Lowery brought symbolic gifts and called the Memphis gathering a historic occasion for the city. Lowery said everyone needed to hear the message of self-reliance and "we need to take the message back to others." Former mayor Dr. Willie W. Herenton was a prominent figure at the leadership conference and at the Sunday event. Farrakhan said Herenton had earned the support he should receive in his bid to become the Ninth District representative and noted that as mayor, Herenton had the courage to present him with the key to the city. (Ajanaku 2009)

On Sunday, Herenton said it was easy to extend the key to Farrakhan, whom he described as worthy, a man who speaks the truth and who is anointed and committed to improving the human condition.

In comments to the crowd before the speech, [Memphis Mayor Willie] Herenton recalled presenting [Nation of Islam leader Louis] Farrakhan with a key to the city despite the controversy it caused.

"It was easy for me as a mayor to present a key ... to a man who is worthy, to a man who speaks truth, to a man who possesses wisdom, to a man who is courageous in thought and in action," said Herenton, who was the first elected black mayor of Memphis. "To an anointed man." (Schelzig 2009)

Chicago Tribune Editorial Page Editor, Don Wycliff

All his hatreds aside, one thing is clear about Farrakhan: He loves black people. He loves them so much that he has made himself hated by virtually every other group in this nation to prove his love for blacks. He loves them so much that he will criticize them as no white person and dam few black people could. Indeed, he boasted about that in his overlong (but far more coherent than most critics gave it credit for being) speech at the Million Man March. "I point out the evils of black people like no other leader does," Farrakhan declared, "but my people don't call me anti-black, because they know I must love them in order to point out what's wrong so we can get it right to come back into the favor of God. One other thing also is certain: Farrakhan, a Muslim, employs Christian and Judaic religious themes more effectively than almost any other prominent contemporary preacher. He did it to powerful effect in his Million Man March address, and in the process summoned up memories of that old religious tradition of which Dr. King was the greatest exemplar. (Wycliff 1995)

Trumpet Magazine Editor Rhonda McKinney Jones

"Because of the Minister's influence in the African American community, *Trumpet News magazine* honors him this winter at its Sounds of the Shore gala with an Empowerment Award. It seemed a fitting tribute for a storied life well lived. And as our brief interview drew to a close and he thanked me for taking the time to talk to him, I could not help but think the Minister, the

man with whom I had been so casually speaking, truly epitomized greatness."
(Media Matters for America 2008)

Rev. Jeremiah A. Wright

"When Minister Farrakhan speaks, Black America listens," says the Rev. Dr. Jeremiah A. Wright, likening the Minister's influence to the E. F. Hutton commercials of old. "Everybody may not agree with him, but they listen ... His depth on analysis when it comes to the racial ills of this nation is astounding and eye opening He brings a perspective that is helpful and honest.
"Minister Farrakhan will be remembered as one of the 20th and 21st century giants of the African American religious experience," continues Wright. "His integrity and honesty have secured him a place in history as one of the nation's most powerful critics. His love for Africa and African American people has made him an unforgettable force, a catalyst for change and a religious leader who is sincere about his faith and his purpose." (Media Matters for America 2008)

Former economic adviser to Pres. Ronald Reagan and Wall Street Guru, Jude Wanniski

"I believe Minister Farrakhan is the most important Muslim leader in the world, who can best represent the concerns of the Islamic world to our government. I have spent countless hours with him...I told him this morning that no one had yet come forward with proof that he ever said, 'Judaism is a gutter religion,' or 'dirty religion,' as I have an outstanding offer of $1000 to anyone who can." (The American Prospect 2002)

ACLC President Archbishop George A. Stallings

Speaking to fellow pastors following Minister Farrakhan's message, ACLC-USA's national co-president Archbishop George Augustus Stallings, remarked that he noticed many taking "copious notes," probably in preparation for Sunday morning sermons. Archbishop Stallings said Min.

Farrakhan had a "Triple A rating" meaning "anointed, appointed and approved" and was "a prophetic voice for our time and age."

"I wish that we as Christian ministers would know the Qur'an the way the Minister knows the scriptures. I wish that we as Christian ministers would get out of our Eurocentric, hegemonic superiority attitude, embracing a religion that is a stolen legacy, rather than celebrating its Afrocentric roots," said Archbishop Stallings.

"I wish that some of us would seek to purify our Christianity. We cannot purify our Christianity until we study the Qur'an. I know that's a shocking statement to some of you Christian folks, but you and I cannot appreciate the true heritage of Christianity until we know the Qur'an, until we know Muhammad (PBUH) until we can articulate the principles of the Islamic faith the way the Hon. Louis Farrakhan articulated the principles of the Christian faith, and not only the Christian faith but also the Jewish faith," Archbishop Stallings added. (A. Muhammad, Farrakhan to spiritual leaders: 'God has never done His greatest work in politics' 2009)

Archbishop George Augustus Stallings, Jr., national president of the American Clergy Leadership Conference, said he admires Minister Farrakhan because he leads by example, and is a man of principle, at a time when many spiritual leaders sacrifice principle for popularity.

"The sterling quality that I appreciate most about the Honorable Minister Louis Farrakhan is that he is uncompromising when it comes to spiritual principles and he does not base his message on what will tickle the ear or what is popular to receive an applause," Archbishop Stallings told *The Final Call*. "What is more important to him is principle rather than power. It is service rather than being served. And it is his ability to challenge all of us to be the watchmen and the watchwomen that we accepted the call to be when we were ordained and yet maybe have fallen by the wayside." (A. Muhammad, Farrakhan delivers a warning and offers a healing for spiritual leaders and humanity 2011)

Torah Jewish Group Neturei Karta

In an historic Feb. 28 announcement, the rabbis told the world of their support for Min. Farrakhan and the Nation of Islam during a press conference after the Saviours' Day weekend celebration.

"We've had hours and hours of conversations with Minister Farrakhan, "said Rabbi David Weiss, "Minister Farrakhan is a strong-willed person. The Jews misconstrued his statements. They (Zionists) changed Judaism with their new style. This is Zionism. Judaism is not like this."

Rabbi Weiss led a delegation of rabbis that were invited to Saviours' Day by Min. Farrakhan as part of their ongoing dialogue and reconciliation. The rabbis spoke throughout the weekend and addressed the capacity crowd at the United Center on Feb. 27.

"Zionism is a transformation from godliness to materialism," explained Rabbi Weiss. "Know the difference between Zionism and Judaism. We are diametrically opposed. We apologize for those who attacked Minister Farrakhan. Those who attacked represent the façade of Judaism."

This example of peace and reconciliation has not been received by all as good news for the faithful. On the contrary, so-called mainstream Jewish groups have attacked this bond as insincere.

In news reports Michael Siegel, president of the Chicago Board of Rabbis, said that "the Jewish community is fairly well-organized and there are bodies equipped to have a conversation. (Farrakhan) knows their phone numbers and the fact that he chose to go elsewhere shows the lack of sincerity" in his outreach.

But the rabbis pointed out that Min. Farrakhan has made outreach for dialogue with his attackers.

Their own relationship with the Nation began last summer when they approached the Muslims seeking help in securing the release of several Jewish rabbis held in Iran for alleged spying.

That led to additional meetings to foster a better relationship. "This Jewish community is an excellent example of how Black and Jewish relations can be," said Nation of Islam Chief of Staff Leonard F. Muhammad.

Before the 1984 elections there was hardly a mumbling word about Min. Farrakhan and Jews. The waters were parted with the great divide when Min. Farrakhan defended Rev. Jackson against Jews seeking to "ruin" his campaign. Those Jews labeled the Minister a new "Hitler."

Although Min. Farrakhan condemned Hitler as being wicked for his deeds, somewhere and somehow that message got deleted from the media reports and all that was played over and over in the press was that Min. Farrakhan called Hitler great.

The next media distortion was the misinterpretation of the following quote: "Now, that nation of Israel never has had any peace in 40 years, and she will never have any peace because there can never be any peace structured on injustice, thievery, lying and deceit and using the name of God to shield your dirty religion under His holy and righteous name."

Again, the media had a field day with that and soon all that was reported was that Min. Farrakhan called Judaism a "gutter religion."

In their new pamphlet, "Exile and Redemption: The Torah Approach, An Introductory Exploration of Zionism, Jewish-Gentile Relations and the Recent Dialogue with the Nation of Islam by a Friend of Neturei Karta, " that remark is explained by Jews themselves.

"The media widely reported that the Minister had referred to Judaism as a 'gutter religion.' This error (or distortion) was deeply troubling to the Nation of Islam. The reason was that in Minister Farrakhan's vocabulary the phrase 'dirty religion' has a particular meaning. It referred to adherents of a faith who sinned against the tenets of that faith. The 'dirty religion' is the distorted faith which emerges from its manipulation by hypocrites or sinners.... The use of 'dirty religion' in the Minister's lexicon could have been discovered by any researcher interested in generating light instead of heat," the statement reads. (N. I. Muhammad 2000)

Former U.S. Representative and HUD Secretary Jack Kemp

"But Kemp also said he so admired the Million Man March organized by Farrakhan last year, and the speech Farrakhan delivered at the event, that he wished he had been able to take part. "That Million Man March was a celebration of responsible fatherhood, individual initiative, of not asking the government to do everything for you, and getting an opportunity to be the man that God meant you to be," Kemp, 61 said. "I would have liked to have been invited to speak." Kemp, a former U.S. Secretary of Housing and Urban Development and one of the few nationally recognized Republicans to consistently focus on the problems faced by minorities and the poor, acknowledged the risk he was taking in praising Farrakhan's emphasis on black self-reliance and family values." (Rezendes 1996)

Former EEOC Chairman and U.S. Supreme Court Justice Clarence Thomas

President Bush's nominee for the Supreme Court, Judge Clarence Thomas, expressed admiration for the Rev. Louis Farrakhan in speeches eight years ago. But Judge Thomas said today that he never shared any of the clergyman's anti-Semitic views. The content of the speeches was disclosed today by The Dallas Times Herald. After leaders of Jewish organizations and civil rights advocates expressed concern about Mr. Thomas's remarks, he issued a statement saying he was not an anti-Semite.

Mr. Farrakhan, the Black Muslim leader, became notorious in 1984 when he spoke of Judaism as "a dirty religion" and described Hitler as "wickedly great." Leaders of Jewish organizations said Mr. Farrakhan had been making anti-Semitic statements at least since 1972.In two speeches prepared for his use in 1983, Mr. Thomas, then chairman of the Equal Employment Opportunity Commission, described Mr. Farrakhan as "a man I have admired for more than a decade." The speeches were for a meeting of the Capital Press Club here on Sept. 19, 1983, and for a meeting of the national Association of Black M.B.A.'s in Atlanta on Oct. 6, 1983. Mr. Thomas quoted Mr. Farrakhan on the need for self-help among blacks, without mentioning any of the minister's views of Judaism. (Pear 1991)

Hip-Hop Mogul and Entrepreneur Russell Simmons

Minister Louis Farrakhan: My Second Father
"When we think of Minister Louis Farrakhan, we often think about the man who helped guide Muhammad Ali or the man who came up together in the Nation of Islam with Malcolm X. Do we ever think he's the man who helped hundreds of thousands (or even millions) of black people to love themselves? Well, we should.

When I grew up in Hollis, Queens there was a rehab, a mosque and a "Steak n' Take" on my corner, all of which were run by the Nation of Islam. There was also a heroin epidemic on that corner that was killing off our teenagers and young adults. Our parents would tell us that when we grow up we should make a choice to either join the army or "be a Muslim or something." The Nation of Islam secured our housing projects, promoted dignity and transformed men with criminal pasts. Those men would then, in turn, raise refined, educated black children. Hard to dispute this. It took guys off the street and created a powerful, non-violent movement. The Nation of Islam has never been associated with any form of violence and always been about uplifting our communities and making a better future for black people. If you ask anyone from my generation, from any ghetto in this country, I promise you they have roughly the same experiences regarding the Nation's presence in their communities.

Certainly some of their preachers were fiery, especially in their pointing out the evils of white supremacy. They said some things in a way that was hard for most whites and some blacks to digest. For example, "THE WHITE MAN IS THE DEVIL." We have to remember the climate of the country during this time. It was an all-out war and the Nation was not about to back-down. The Nation of Islam, which was started by Elijah Muhammad and a white man named, Master Fard Muhammad, always pointed out that one day we would all live in harmony. Although this still isn't quite true, their message under the leadership of Minister Louis Farrakhan has evolved to fit the time.

It is true that some blacks are still not "free" and stuck in a slave mentality, due to the lingering effects of 400+ years of slavery. It is the recognition of this condition that the Nation continues its important work in ghettos across America, giving steady doses of spirituality or sense of higher self to many men and women who need it.

This past week, it was my honor to host the Honorable Minister Louis Farrakhan at my apartment in NYC. He was joined by his sons Louis Jr., Mustapha and Joshua Farrakhan, along with their personal chef and at least 75 security personnel. It was quite a scene to see how they set up shop at my apartment. This was a week where I didn't miss my 6 am prayer because I could hear them already awake and ready to start the day off right. This was a week where the word "Allah" was on the tip of everyone's tongue. And was a very special time when I got to hang with my "second dad" and my other brothers. We reminisced about the three marches where more than three million people marched on Washington. We talked about how we brought Snoop, Ice Cube and other LA rappers together with members of the east coast rap community and how he helped mediate the beef between 50 Cent and Ja Rule and countless other instances where he was there to help hip hop. And of course we talked about his keynote address at the hip hop summit that created the Hip Hop Summit Action network. We even mentioned a subject that the Minister doesn't care to discuss, his legacy. He has talked about the oneness of god for years, about the sameness of all religion and all people. He has given his followers spiritual roadmaps to happiness on Earth his whole life. I want future generations to know him as I do, so I am working to have his thoughts on this subject made into a book. I believe that his memoirs are going to be one of the most interesting and inspiring autobiographies ever written.

So that is my goal.

If America can know his heart, it will inspire millions of Americans for generations to come. It will happen with or without me, but I just thought writing this would be a good karmic expression for me, and a chance to reflect on a very special few days in my life. (Simmons 2009)

Rapper 50 Cent

I never met my father, right. But if I had the opportunity to pick a father, ah, man   I'd probably pick...who would I pick man?...I'd pick Minister Farrakhan...I would. Minister Farrakhan would be a cool father; like 'Minister Farrakhan my pops nigga, don't play with me I'll pop off.' (G-Unit Radio 19 2013)

R&B Vocalist Stephanie Mills

"He's a great man, I think he's misunderstood in a lot of ways, but I think he's a great man. And I am happy that he's been able to endure." (Black Entertainment Television 2003)

Rev. Jesse L. Jackson Sr.

"Average people follow a path; leaders of significance carve a trail where there was no path, to that extent the Minister is a trailblazer...No one speaks to them more powerfully and more consistently than Minister Louis Farrakhan...His being alive is a miracle unto itself, he just refuses to surrender; his spirit, his body, his religion, he keeps on fighting back." (Black Entertainment Television 2003)

Professor Michael Eric Dyson

"And despite the outer perimeters of controvery that attach to Minister Farrakhan, I think Black people always understood that this was a man who loved Black people, who engaged Black people where they lived, and long before rap singers where talking about keeping it real, Minister Farrakhan was speaking truth to power... His ability to tell what's on his mind that most Black people love him for, because we have so many leaders who kowtow and genuflect before the shrine of popularity, who don't want to speak their mind because they think it might hurt their bottom line...For the first time in African American history; a non-Christian leader is a significant, if not the significant leader within Black America" (Black Entertainment Television 2003)

Elma Lewis, friend of the Minister's mother

"He was the jewel of the neighborhood really, in the church and school, wherever he went; he had a real talent for lighting up the world." (Black Entertainment Television 2003)

Pastor of St. Sabina Church and Community Activist Father Michael Pfleger

"He has–first of all; he has not called Judaism a gutter religion of blood suckers. That is not what he has said because I have heard that talk. I stick up for Louis Farrakhan because he is another person that the media has chosen to define how they want to do it. And they demonize how they want to demonize somebody. I know the man, Louis Farrakhan. He is a great man. I have great respect for him; he has done an awful lot for people and this country, black, white, and brown. He's a friend of mine." (O'Reilly 2008)

Journalist Gregory Kane

What I'm about to say will no doubt get me in trouble with the Jewish community. Protesters will have to stand in line. They can queue up behind my friends in the Nation of Islam, where perhaps they will come to a meeting of the minds on at least one issue.

Because the truth is there is much about Farrakhan and the Nation of Islam that is praiseworthy. Comparisons to Hitler and Mussolini for making the trains run on time don't begin to describe the nature of the Nation of Islam's work. Carlos Muhammad of Baltimore's Mosque No. 6 pointed to one NOI member who, before he joined, was a crack addict.

Reaching out to redeem drug addicts and others filled with hopelessness has been part of the NOI's mission for years. If Louis Farrakhan sends his ministers out into the streets to help save such people, he deserves praise, not condemnation. Funny, isn't it, how those of us who have viciously vilified the man over the years are now shamefully silent about the allegation of the San Jose Mercury News that it was indeed the CIA that backed a group that introduced crack to Los Angeles, triggering an epidemic that spread across the nation. We excoriate the man fighting to end it and say not one negative comment about the ones who may have helped start it.

Earlier this year, Farrakhan told Mike Wallace of the television show "60 Minutes" that America was the most corrupt society on earth. If the CIA/crack story is true, it turns out that Farrakhan was on the mark. Don't you loathe him when he's right?

We loathe him when he's right and wrong, and in spite of the clearly good things his organization has done in the impoverished areas of urban black America. But if we apply moral absolutism in the case of Louis Farrakhan, let's be fair and apply it to everybody.

Because the CIA may have helped flood America's streets with crack, let's conclude that America's government is evil and incapable of being reformed. Because former Mossad agent Victor Ostrovsky charged that the Israeli intelligence agency recruited three Palestinians to assassinate former President George Bush; executed the would-be assassins when the plot failed; did indeed assassinate British media magnate Robert Maxwell; and used Palestinians and blacks in Soweto, South Africa, as guinea pigs in biological and chemical warfare experiments, the government of Israel must be inherently evil.

We won't do that, of course. We'd much prefer to bask in the rays of our own self-righteousness, not even acknowledging that next to those good ol' boys in the Mossad, the Nation of Islam leader looks downright saintly. Louis Farrakhan, we charge, is anti-Semitic, bigoted, intolerant and intransigent.

But it looks like his most vocal critics may be guilty of some intolerance and intransigence of our own. (Kane 1996)

Haki R. Madhubuti

That Minister Farrakhan had the vision, organization, money, independence and spiritual strength to stand up against gangsta odds and say, "let's meet in Washington," and to reach out to the Black church, Black fraternal organizations, Black professional organizations, Black women organizations, Black Nationalists and Pan-Africans, Black college students and Black street people all across the country was definitely an act of humility, spiritual growth, inclusion and political insight. (Karenga and Madhubuti 1996, 68)

Dr. Cornel West

Needless to say, Minister Louis Farrakhan was brilliant, gracious and open as was his wife, Khadijah...Since this substantive meeting I have been trashed by many (some former friends and acquaintances) and eschewed by others. And in the eyes of some in the Jewish world, I've met and collaborated with the new Hitler. This is sheer nonsense- and part of the problem. When Black people sit and talk with their white adversaries, they are praised. When Martin Luther King preached that he loved such white supremacists as Bull Connor, the white media showered him with approval and admiration. When Black people trash and denounce other Black leaders-demonized by the white media-they are praised. But when Black people who disagree in public decide to meet in private-all of us are trashed and denounced. When Martin Luther King preached that he loved Elijah Muhammad-and met with him in private-the white media denounced him. The double standards and differential treatment-the core of white supremacy-are evident.

My support of the Million Man March and dialogue with Minister Louis Farrakhan is based on neither blood nor race. As a radical democrat and, most importantly, Christian, my support and dialogue are based on spiritual, moral and political grounds. Spiritual because I view each and every one of us as, human beings made in the image of God capable of growth, development and maturity. Hence, I give up on no one of us-we are all in process, in need of one another. Morally, because though I believe patriarchal, homophobic and anti-Jewish sentiments are wretched sins, we all must be pushed to minimize the evils in all of us. None of us are pure and pristine, free of sin and evil. Yet we grow, develop and mature owing to loving criticism, not hateful castigation. Politically, I am convinced that white supremacy is the major dam holding back the progressive energies in the American body politic. If we can target white supremacy, then the other crucial issues of poverty, mal-distribution of wealth, corporate power, patriarchy, homophobia and ecological abuse will be brought into daylight. Why so? Because race matters so much in American society. (Karenga and Madhubuti 1996)

Alice Walker

I can't imagine becoming Muslim...I did not think Farrakhan was proselytizing...I was moved by his apparent humility; and underneath all the trappings of Islam, which I personally find frightening, I glimpsed a man of humor, a persuasive teacher and someone unafraid to speak truth to power, a virtue that makes it easier to be patient as he struggles to subdue his flaws. (Karenga and Madhubuti 1996, 42)

Selwyn Seyfu Hinds

Farrakhan's self-help doctrine hardly resembles hollow right-wing platitudes. The right's practice of telling folks to pull themselves up is coupled with vicious attacks on the structures that lend them a modicum of support, while Farrakhan's is fleshed out by tangible outreach into the meanest streets and souls of besieged Black America. In this way, of this afternoon, Farrakhan has reached me. (Karenga and Madhubuti 1996, 64)

Ron Daniels

Minister Louis Farrakhan more than any other leader in this period has captured the imagination of Black America precisely because of his steadfast denunciation of racism and white supremacy and his persistent call for moral and spiritual renewal, self-reliance and self-determination. Though Minister

Farrakhan has remarkable appeal across classes and constituencies within the Black America, his appeal among the poor and disadvantaged is unrivaled. Hence, the enormous response to the Million Man March/Day of Atonement among people who have not been attracted to or participated in any mass action in their lifetime. When Farrakhan made the call for the Million Man March/Day of Atonement, the masses responded.

Obviously, anyone who can issue a call for a Million Man March/Day of Atonement and get massive response becomes a leader to be reckoned with within Black America. Minister Farrakhan, therefore, emerges as the pre-eminent African American leader in this period. (Karenga and Madhubuti 1996, 108)

Dr. Charshee McIntyre and Dr. Barbara Sizemore

Dr. Charshee McIntyre cited Dr. Barbara Sizemore, the eminent educator and currently Dean at DePaul University in Chicago, as another associate who strongly endorses the march. "She told me that the Nation of Islam is the best group in the country for the development of Black men, for instilling unity and camaraderie, and I agree," McIntyre said. "And as women become more educated you'll notice that they are rising to prominence within the Nation, and that to me is a natural progression." (Karenga and Madhubuti 1996, 114)

Dr. Geneva Smitherman

Quiet as it's kept, Farrakhan is respected by millions of African American, on all socio-economic levels, for his courage in standing up to an oppressive system and his penchant for calling white folk out. Truly "unbought and unbossed," he often says the things that many Blacks feel but don't have the freedom to express. According to a poll reported in Time, 59% of Blacks believe Farrakhan is a good role model for Black youth and that he speaks the truth. Since the March, some Black folk have started saying things like: "Now, I tell you what the problem is with her son, even though it's gon hurt, cause I'm like Farrakhan, uhma tell the truth." (Karenga and Madhubuti 1996, 104)

Journalist and Publisher of Emerge Magazine George Curry

Despite all the criticism enveloping Farrakhan, the Million Man March was a stunning success. There was a sense of love and brotherhood that cannot be adequately conveyed to those who chose to stay away. Man after man said, "Pass the love," as they gently pounded one another's fists. They even passed money to total strangers. Now the challenge is to take that love and trust, and spread it among our respective communities. (Karenga and Madhubuti 1996, 128)

Journalist and Activist Kevin Powell

"God knows, when I heard Farrakhan, I had never heard a black man talk like that. It blew my mind, absolutely blew my mind, It was intoxicating, as intoxicating as crack was for a lot of people in our community in the '80s. (Cheney 2005)"

Musician and Composer James Mtume

Well first and foremost, I think he's the only person or personality that the hip hop community respects...I've seen his symphonic work and I think personally that's one of the things that really separates him from many of the other so-called leaders. I personally believe that true leadership has to be connected to some artistic sensibility and he more than anyone else demonstrates that. (Black Entertainment Television 2003)

Actor Bernie Casey

What he primarily proselytizes, I think all Black Americans agree with, which is to be stand up men, responsible men, men that are dependable that take care of their families, that respect their wives and children, that try to get gainful employment, to be a help to the community; all those things. How could you possibly object to that? (Black Entertainment Television 2003)

College Friend Clarence "Jeep" Jones

Some don't have the courage to say the things they believe even though in our hearts we think it; I know I think some of the things that he said. Would I have the courage to say them, I 'm not sure.-Clarence "Jeep" Jones. (Black Entertainment Television 2003)

Brother Wayne Grice

When he would give us (his staff) something to do or share his vision, he was always open to our natural and real reaction and we were free enough, he gave us freedom to say what was really on our mind. (Black Entertainment Television 2003)

President Bill Clinton

Former President Bill Clinton said that he supports the efforts of African American leaders who are organizing the Millions More March, a national gathering of Blacks scheduled to take place in October in Washington, D.C, a decade after the Million Man March was convened.

In a rare interview at his Harlem office with the Amsterdam News earlier this week, Clinton said that the gathering--publicly announced last Monday by Minister Louis Farrakhan, Rev. Al Sharpton, and Rev. Jesse L. Jackson--could train a positive spotlight on critical issues impacting African Americans.

"I think this is a very positive idea," said Clinton, who spoke to the Amsterdam News on his first full day back in his office since his second operation due to complications following his quadruple bypass surgery last September. "I think the country's focus understandably has strayed a little over the last few years," Clinton said, adding that while America should focus on homeland security, it must also solve the racial and economic disparity that still exists.

Clinton, who remains extremely popular among African Americans, said that another march, followed by aggressive organizing efforts, could help to curtail some of the challenges in the Black community, which range from high unemployment and alarming prison rates.

"Jesse [Jackson] and Mr. [Louis] Farrakhan and Rev. [Al] Sharpton probably have internal domestic political differences, but they've agreed on this and I think it's a good thing," said Clinton. "I like the idea of a march, but I think it would also be good at the march for them to say, 'We want to call your attention to this problem and here's something else you can do. And that it's fine to be concerned about [homeland] security, but we also have to keep trying to make America strong and better here at home. And we can't neglect the quality of our jobs, the quality of our education, the quality of our environment.'"

The event, scheduled to take place in October, is expected to draw millions of African Americans to the nation's capital for the three days to participate in a Day of Absence from work and school on Friday, Oct 14, followed by a march on Oct. 15, and religious services the next day.

Clinton said that he supported the Million Man March a decade ago, adding that the gathering was a powerful symbolic expression.

"They were basically standing up for the dignity of family and asking African American men and fathers to be more responsible," Clinton said. "It was totally non-violent and got a big participation and it also showed frankly, a face to a part of America that is not as sympathetic to the problems that African Americans in the cities and the poor rural areas have ... that hey, there's all these people and they are advocating a responsible agenda and not just asking for something, and they're saying, 'This is our responsibility; this is what we're supposed to do.' I personally thought it was quite positive." (Watson 2005)

U.S. Representative James Traficant

James Traficant (D-Ohio) praised the march, in a one-minute speech. "I attended the Million Man March," he said, "I thought it was the right thing to do." He said that "the message was powerful. The themes were responsible: self-responsibility, economic independence, morality, love, parenthood. Those are good messages for all America." He concluded that "there is reality here. The Pope and Billy Graham are great human beings, but the Pope and Billy Graham and all the religious leaders of the world will not solve the race problem in America. It is going to; in fact, require the help of all people. Congress should join in and commend that march. It was good for the country." (Osgood 1995)

LaWanna Mayfield

The following is an excerpt of an interview with LaWanna Mayfield conducted by Matt Comer. Ms. Mayfield is a Charlotte, NC city councilperson who appeared at a leadership meeting held by the Honorable Minister Louis Farrakhan during the Holy Day of Atonement observance in October 2012. Ms. Mayfield was pressured by media outlets within the city of Charlotte to renounce the Minister. She refused and stood resolutely by her decision to attend the meeting.

What do you say to people who want you to publicly denounce Farrakhan?
[The] same thing I said at the beginning. It's God's place to judge people. The great thing about the United States is everyone has an opinion, and I represent an extremely diverse community. It is not my place to place judgment on anyone. I'm not God, and I don't intend to be.

Would you consider denouncing Farrakhan based on his anti-LGBT and anti-Semitic remarks?
It is your responsibility as an individual, as an adult and as a young adult to not listen to everything one person says. We need to be individual thinkers, so I'm going to look at the good people have done and I'm going to look at where we can build something together as opposed to focusing on our differences. At the end of the day, there are things I do not agree with, but I also recognize, as an African-American female, a lot has been done for the African-American community by the Muslim community under the leadership of Minister Farrakhan.

Is there a tipping point where Farrakhan's beliefs are harmful versus helpful?
I am African American first before I am anything else. Every room I walk into, before you identify my sexuality, before you know I'm an elected official,

before you know where I went to school, what you see is an African-American female.

The day I was born, my ethnicity was stated on my birth certificate. The day I die, that's what's going to be on my birth certificate. It is not going to say whether or not I was heterosexual, lesbian, bi or transsexual. I'm going to continue to be as respectful to as many people as I possibly can be, but I'm not going to shy away from who I am as an African-American female.

I am not going to discount the work Minister Farrakhan has done any more than I would discount the work I have done in the Latino, Asian Pacific and other diverse communities. I'm not going to let anyone bully me into taking a stance I don't personally believe in.

How would you explain your position to an LGBT person in your community?

Very few people have asked me. When MeckPAC was called to denounce me, they did not. When [the national Gay & Lesbian] Victory Fund was called to denounce me, they did not. I am doing exactly what I said I would do and represent everyone, not get side-tracked because one or two people feel like I should take a stance without having had any real conversation about the totality of an individual.

The Southern Poverty Law Center calls the Nation a hate group.

Are we saying Muslims are hateful? How many Muslims follow the leadership of Minister Farrakhan? I'm not concerned with anything other than what I was there in attendance for; to participate in an African-American leadership discussion.

Do you think Southern Poverty Law Center's hate-group designation is inaccurate?

For me, the hate group designation has as much merit as those of us in the community who think all Muslims are terrorists. It's that type of intolerance that encourages "us versus them," as opposed to encouraging communities to work together. (Comer 2012)

Jeffrey Steinberg

The largest peaceful demonstration in American history, the "Million Man March" which gathered at the foot of the U. S. Capitol on Monday, Aug. 16, has changed politics in the United States and effectively reflected the growing disgust of the American public with the Conservative Revolution of House Speaker Newt Gingrich and his allies. The rally was built around a call for a national "Day of Atonement" issued by Minister Louis Farrakhan, the head of the Nation of Islam, who called last year for 1 million black men to come to Washington, D.C. (Steinberg 1995)

Kweisi Mfume

"We want the word to go forward today to friend and foe alike that the Congressional Black Caucus, after having entered into a sacred covenant with the NAACP [National Association

for the Advancement of Colored People) to work for real and meaningful change, will enter into that same covenant with the Nation of Islam," said CBC Chairman Rep. Kweisi Mfume (D-Md.). The Nation of Islam in Washington, D.C. has gained a well-deserved reputation for their effectiveness in cleaning up housing complexes overrun by the drug trade, generally recognized as the number-one threat to the black community, and has also played a prominent role in the fight against AID S. In a declaration of unity that brought a standing ovation from the 3,500 people in attendance at the meeting at the Washington Convention Center, Mfume said, "No longer will we allow people to divide us." CBC membership increased 50% in the last election.-by William Jones (W. Jones 1993)

Andrew Young

Atlanta Mayor Andrew Young, U.S. ambassador to the United Nations under Jimmy Carter, interviewed by the Baltimore Jewish Times on Aug. 30, said he agrees with "nine tenths" of what Nation of Islam leader Louis Farrakhan says. Farrakhan, who has made frequent anti-Semitic remarks, is on the receiving end of millions from Libyan dictator Muammar Qaddafi, and has also characterized himself as an admirer of Adolf Hitler. Young calls Farrakhan a "legitimate player in the mainstream of black ideas" and says his POWER plan is "wonderful . . . because it would employ lots of people." Young insisted that he "has never heard him say anything against the Jews." Asked how he would feel if the situation were reversed, and the Ku Klux Klan were advocating race hatred against blacks, Young replied, "I have always said that the Ku Klux Klan is made up of poor white people who are part of the mainstream of America's social and political life, and they need to be helped, not hated." (Executive Intelligence Review 1985)

Debra Hanania-Freeman

Farrakhan used the opportunity to release a statement entitled "A Torchlight For America," whose text was excerpted from his forthcoming book of the same title, to be released sometime in May. Farrakhan's remarks examined the status of the nation's health care system, welfare reform, taxation, prison reform, the national debt, and the economy. Although the speech was packed with facts and statistics, and was bitingly accurate in its critique of the state of the U. S. economy, what was most striking about the presentation was not Minister Farrakhan's acumen as an economist, but his personal vision of God, his good humor, and the kind of passionate defense of African Americans that could only be delivered by one who has fully internalized his own responsibility to provide leadership for his people....Hearing Farrakhan in person for the first time was clearly startling to many of those gathered who had only read news accounts of him circulated by his enemies. But Farrakhan's wit, vitality, and most importantly, his humanity, were irrepressible. Farrakhan is, without question, a far different man than the sound-bite target that the Anti-Defamation League (ADL) of B'nai B'rith has constructed. Indeed, he thanked Lyndon LaRouche's associates for their work and insights exposing the ADL, saying; he was shocked when he saw the ADL's "Farrakhan dossier" portraying him and those associated with him as criminals. Clearly, Farrakhan came to Washington to deliver a message and to offer his help to a troubled nation. He is a national asset whose voice should be heard. (Freeman 1993)

Fredrick Allen

Frederick Allen, columnist for the Atlanta Journal/Constitution, titled his Thanksgiving Day column, "Farrakhan's Real Message Has Validity." "Where other leaders invariably make blacks feel helpless, [Nation of Islam leader

Louis] Farrakhan offers hope. ...anti-Semitism is not the source of his appeal, and for this we can be thankful," Allen wrote. (Allen 1985)

Professor Derrick Bell

Anything out of the accepted is seen as a problem, by an awful lot of us. When Lewis Farrakhan speaks to his audience he upsets a hell of a lot of white people, you see. But while he is speaking to the needs and the hopes and what have you, of the people to whom he is speaking, and that's just going to happen. I see Lewis Farrakhan as a great hero for the people. I don't agree with everything he says, and some of his tactics, but hell, I don't agree with everything anybody says. (MacNeil Lehr News Hour 2012)

Smart and super articulate, Minister Farrakhan is perhaps the best living example of a black man ready, willing and able to 'tell it like it is' regarding who is responsible for racism in this country .... Every black person important enough to be interviewed is asked to condemn Minister Farrakhan--or any other truly outspoken black leader. (Bell 1993)

Journalist Clarence Page

Clarence Page, one of the best-known and most admired African American commentators, described his experience in Washington as therapeutic. "Since black men, particularly young black males, are the most feared and loathed creatures on urban streets today, we need self-esteem more than most." To recognize that it was Farrakhan who called the march and who pulled it off is not to condone Farrakhan's rhetoric. As Page notes, "Those who refuse to acknowledge the ability of blacks to support the march without supporting Farrakhan refuse to allow blacks the right to be diverse or the ability to be complicated.... I wish a black leader who was less incendiary than Louis Farrakhan had issued the call for black men to come out to the Million Man March. But they didn't and he did. He stuck his neck out and it paid off. It was his day. Give it to him. (Wall 1995)

Poet and Writer Nikki Giovanni

I BELIEVE that old virus, racism, is still running rampant in our community, but I think we may have found an antidote in the Million Man March. I think one of the most important movements of this decade took place on October 16, 1995 in Washington, DC. That hundreds of thousands (though I believe a million plus) Black men came together to commune, to atone, to simply be close to each other and absorb some love and some support from each other was a great, historic event.

I am not expecting either Minister Farrakhan or the million men to create any miracles. We all, men and women, are just people trying our best to make sense of our lives. But I feel that by standing up, a great shaking of the earth occurred. There was no grandstanding. There were no putdowns of folk who were scared to go. There was a positive feeling that men needed to do something to affirm their existence.

As a Black woman, as a Christian, as a citizen of Planet Earth, I simply believe we all have to not only acknowledge but rejoice that the men are moving. If Black women alone could save this planet, then it would have been done. We need our friend, our partner, our son to stand with us. Before they can stand at our side they needed to take measure of each other.

This is a wonderful calling that Louis Farrakhan caused. I am sure everyone noted that Bill Clinton had not stood up to any Republican demand until after the March when he finally found his backbone.

I am very happy for the men. They will need to continue to touch base with each other, to cooperate with each other, to love and care for each other in the future. They may or may not have another march. I believe the one that they had will be sustaining. I know, if I may quote my own poetry, "... Walking down the street is the same old danger... But a brand new pleasure." (Giovanni 1996)

Snoop Dogg (Lion) Rapper/Actor

And it was exactly around the time that I (seek) the information from Minister Farrakhan, because we never had a leader, but we could always depend on Minister Louis Farrakhan because he understood us. And he spoke my language; he never talked bad about us. He always encouraged us. So we always respected him. And, when it got bad, I reached out to him. And he accepted me with warm arms and he had me come out to his house. ... The Minister has always been there for the hip-hop community. I want to tell yall 'bout a story, that takes too much time but, it was about 10 years ago, when the rapper Notorious Biggie got killed in Los Angeles. I put a call out to Minister Farrakhan and we put a gathering where all of the rappers came together and we ended all of our beefs and we all had peace and it was love, and we been living that way ever since then. And that's all I've been on, peace, love and positivity – anybody that know me. When I went to go see Minister Farrakhan over 11 years ago; he gave me my mission to go do that. And I've been on it. I've been organizing and bringing the rappers together being the main advocate for peace. Just doing my thang and never really knowing why, but just doing it. So now it's like it came to a catapult, with like where this is why you're doing this. This is the reason why. It's always been in you, now let it out. (Lion 2013)

Boxing Heavyweight Champion Mike Tyson

Larry King – Uh, what do you think that is going out there in the world with the Farracans (Farrakhans) and the like?

Mike Tyson – I, personally as a person man, you know what I mean, people differ with me; I absolutely love Farrakhan. I don't know the gentleman by the name Kolod (Khallid) Muhammad. But Farrakhan as a person, I love Farrakhan. And it's very easy for a person to judge someone of what they say, but if you're a wise man, a real man would never have ill feelings (of) the speaker but to take (in) heed of what he says if what he says is true. You know what I mean? You must correct yourself, and if it's not true, you must prevent it from happening.

Larry King – But if he's wrong you should correct him?

Mike Tyson – If the man's wrong, then what he says has no significance.

(Larry King/CNN 2013)

Journalist and Writer Fahizah Alim

"In the NOI, black Americans see a group of proud and fearless black men who follow Minister Farrakhan. Black men who will go into drug and gang infested public housing complexes and confront the lawless. And they see an economic plan to revitalize black families and black communities that have been abandoned by government and corporate entities.

I know Farrakhan's real world impact on people. For example, when I started attending the University of California, Berkley, I also started taking the birth control pill. I think it was included in the registration packet. I mention the birth control pill because at the time, it was the drug of choice for most single young women. Many who were still in high school and not yet sexually active were prescribed the potent drugs, allegedly to "regulate their cycles."

Moreover, marijuana, "drop out," and "free love" were the buzzwords of my generation. The Beatles, Jimi Hendrix, Sly and the Family Stone, our Pied Pipers of modernity, lured us into a dark and swirling hole of hedonism. And Farrakhan, espousing the teachings of Elijah Muhammad, brought me out of the tailspin. Until that point, I had been taking birth control pills to keep from getting pregnant. **But after listening to Louis Farrakhan speak about how potent a drug must be to be capable of shutting down one of nature's powerful biological functions-that of reproducing itself-I stopped.**

It took me another 2 years to ovulate or produce eggs again. And some years later, the pharmaceutical companies revealed that we had been guinea pigs and the pills prescribed to some young women were about 10 times more potent than they should have been.

"You are poisoning yourself," Farrakhan has said. "Why kill the fruit of your womb and prevent maybe another great Black Leader from being born? Hasn't Pharaoh killed enough of our children?" **I am glad I heard him, I stopped taking the pill. And now I am the proud mother of 4 children: a daughter and 3 sons."**

In major cities across the country, Minister Farrakhan is trying to build businesses, open schools, and teach black people how to pool their resources to build something for themselves...But, most important, he loves black people. [He] loves them more than he loves white people. And that is a rare black person to find. Most "black leaders" want to appease white folks. They need to have their intellect, their humanity, their worthiness validated by white people-the same people brought up to despise them. But not Farrakhan. That is his appeal.

As an NOI lieutenant during the 1970s, my task was teaching and training the women who joined the organization. I witnessed young chemically addicted female prostitutes come out of the drug culture and become good, loving mothers and homemakers. I saw former alcoholics and hustlers, wayward men and cheats become honest, dependable, and hard-working family men. I saw radical anarchists become community builders and schoolteachers. I even saw men involved in homosexual activity become satisfied husbands and fathers. This was done by a belief system and program that told them that their humanity did not originate in slavery or the jungles of Africa.

For me the Nation of Islam was a womb in which I was allowed to flourish and grow, to a point. It served as a womb that sheltered me and allowed me to develop and gain a knowledge of myself absent the presence of white supremacy. In America, blacks need a healthy framework by which we can shape ourselves...I am proud of my experience in the Nation of Islam and glad for the personal evolution it provided me. (Alexander 1998, 161-167)

Fahizah Alim is an award winning columnist for the Sacramento Bee and a former member of the Nation of Islam. The above quote is taken from the book Farrakhan Factor by Amy Alexander

Dr. Aminah McCloud

Now, in the last decade of the twentieth century, while the overall number of traditional black Muslims living in America continues to swell, the realities of the Muslim condition in the world community and the tensions between the ummah and the domestic realm remain constant.

Minister Farrakhan is trying to bridge these two worlds-and link his at-home concerns with the greater ummah. When Farrakhan visits leaders in Iran or Libya, an uniformed observer might see only that the Minister is willfully consorting with America's enemies, rather than recognizing the visit as an expression of his commitment to ummah...

In the same way that the five-times-daily prayers erase one set of class and gender issues, the notion of ummah obscures nation-state borders. This detail is critical in beginning to place some of Farrakhan's thoughts and actions within a larger Islamic context. For instance, by his continual condemnation of neocolonialism on the African continent and in the Caribbean, Louis Farrakhan demonstrates an understanding of the notion of ummah, however unorthodox his methods of expressing this understanding. (Alexander 1998, 175-177)

Dr. Aminah B. McCloud is an associate professor of religious studies at DePaul University. Excerpt from The Farrakhan Factor by Amy Alexander

Imam Warithudeen Mohammed

I introduce the man that left me. He said I got to go out, there are too many going astray, I hate to see them going back to what we pulled them out of with your father's teachings. So I'm going back. Did I ever tell you don't do that? Did I ever tell you don't do that? No, I didn't tell him not to do that. So he went out and he became another leader, new leader of the Nation of Islam, and he has done a marvelous job. Stay with him until you all get to the Promised Land. We embrace him and we are going with Minister Farrakhan all the way to the Promised Land. (Mohammed, Saviours' Day Jumuah Los Angeles 2002)

Imam Warithudeen Mohammed during February 15, 2002 Friday Jumuah Prayer Service during the Saviours' Day Weekend in Los Angeles

Dear Muslim brothers and sisters, it is not difficult for Minister Farrakhan and Wallace D. Mohammed to embrace each other. That's easy for us. When I first met him in the early '50s, I liked him on first sight, and I became his friend and his brother. And I have not stopped being his friend and his brother. Maybe he has not understood the way that I have been his friend and his brother at certain times, but I have always been his friend and his brother. For me this is too big a cause for our personal problems and differences. Allah-u Akbar.

We are to support each other in all good things. When the brother Muslim stands upon the Qur'an, the last of the revealed books and the complete book for all times and all societies, and when he stands upon faith in Muhammad as God's last prophet and Messenger to all the worlds, mercy to all the worlds, we are to support him in that.

As I said, it's easy for me to embrace Minister Farrakhan. Our families are together. We are really one family. Our friendship has not died, and it will not die. And the little problem, the small problem, that we've had along the way, struggling to present ourselves as God willed that we present ourselves, it's not bigger than the word of God, the Qur'an, and (it's) not bigger than Muhammad, the model for all human beings, for all people of faith. It's very small.

So we see, we think, what have we done to bring about this togetherness? What have we done to bring about this closeness that we have this minute? What have we done to free our hearts so we can hug each other and kiss each other, as I did kiss my brother? What have we done to bring that about? Nothing but tried to find the way in the path of Islam, and Allah did the rest. Allah did the rest.

I want to say that Minister Farrakhan is a great leader. I've watched him over the years, since the passing away of my father and our fallen leader, the Honorable Elijah Muhammad. I've watched him and I have done a little mathematics, a little calculation, and I've come up with progress for the

Nation of Islam under the leadership of Minister Farrakhan. Whatever has troubled us in the past, I think we can bury it now and never look back at that grave. And never look back at that grave. (Mohammed, Saviours Day Jumuah 2000)

Imam Warithudeen Mohammed, excerpt from comments delivered by Imam W. Deen Mohammed during Jumu'ah prayer service held Feb. 25, at the McCormick Center as part of the Nation of Islam's Saviours' Day 2000 celebration in Chicago, published in The Final Call Newspaper

Imam Siraj Wahhaj

"Minister Farrakhan holds the key to the development of (Islam) in this country—so we're going to talk about where we go from here, let us now continue the process so that we can move even further on toward the development of Islam in America because the attack is against Islam and they don't ask you the question (are you) Sunni or Shiite, (are) you with the Nation (of Islam) or what? No. We have to recognize that the enemies of Islam are united against us," said Imam Siraj Wahhaj. (A. Muhammad, Life and ministry of Imam W. Deen Mohammed remembered 2008)

Imam Siraj Wahhaj, Amir of Muslim Alliance of North America during the memorial service held for Imam Warithuddin Mohammed. Quote excerpted from in The Final Call Newspaper September 21, 2008 article by Ashahed Muhammad

Henry Louis Gates and Dr. C. Eric Lincoln

Certainly the Farrakhan I met was a model of civility and courtesy. I was reminded of C. Eric Lincoln's account of the last couple of visits he paid to Farrakhan at his home: "Louis insisted on getting down on his hands and knees on the floor to take my shoes off. You know, I'm overweight, and it's a difficult task to get shoes and socks off. And so Louis said, 'I will do that.' And I said, "No, no.' And Louis said, 'No, I want to do it.' He took my shoes off and rubbed my feet to get the blood circulating." I met someone who was eager, even hungry, for conversation; someone of great intelligence who seemed intellectually lonely... In the end, however, it isn't Farrakhan but Farrakhan's following that demands explanation. We might start by admitting the moral authority that Black Nationalism commands even among those blacks who ostensibly disapprove of it. In the village where I grew up, there was a Holiness Church, where people spoke in tongues and fell down in religious ecstasy. It was not my church; my family and I shunned the Pentecostal fervor. And yet, on some level we believed it to be the real thing, realer than our own, more temperate Episcopal services. It was the place to go if you really needed something-if you go desperately sick, say- because the Holy Ghost lived there. (There are Reform Jews who admit to a similar attitude toward their Hasidic brethren.) In this same vein, the assimilated black American, who lives in Scarsdale and drives a Lexus, responds to Farrakhan and Farrakhanism as a presence at once threatening and exhilarating, dismaying and cathartic. (Alexander 1998, 47)

Henry Louis Gates, Jr. is the Alphonse Fletcher University Professor at Harvard University, as well as director of the W.E.B. Du Bois Institute for African and African American Research. Excerpt from The Farrakhan Factor by Amy Alexander

Professor Ernest Allen Jr.

On the positive side of the balance sheet, Louis Farrakhan often provides an exemplary example of black male leadership. He articulates the aspirations of large numbers of African Americans (including our entrepreneurial strata) and speaks out forcefully against incidents of African American oppression. Generally speaking, his internationalism presents a salutary aspect of his leadership as well, a constant reminder that we, as black Americans, must strive to avoid the trap of parochial thinking and steadfastly conceive of solutions to our social and political problems in global terms. Finally, whatever may have been the limitations of the Million Man March, it has provided a catalyst for untold numbers of black men to involve themselves in their local communities, an achievement that cannot be gainsaid even by Farrakhan's most trenchant critics...One of the long-term salutary roles of the NOI, both old and new, has been its demonstrated capacity to resurrect the "fallen" of the race and restore them to productive lives. (Alexander 1998, 87)

Ernest Allen Jr., is an associate professor in the W.E.B. Dubois Department of Afro-American Studies at the University of Massachusetts at Amherst. Excerpted from The Farrakhan Factor by Amy Alexander

Dr. Michael Eric Dyson

The Nation's singular focus on helping black men get their lives together is driven by its ideology of resistance to white supremacy. The Nation has worked diligently to make proud men out of black prisoners, those in jail or those whose self-image is distorted because they are captives to a worship of the white world. The Nation has always seen black male addictions-as symptoms of a virus of lostness that infects the entire black community. The Nation holds that the lostness of black men leads them to abuse their wives and children; to abuse their bodies with alcohol and bad food; to maim and murder each other; and to embrace, like black revolutionary theorist Frantz Fanon, the breasts of white womanhood in search of the milk of affection and affirmation. Long before the decline of black male life became widely apparent; and long before black males were vilified and glamorized by both the cultural right and the left, the Nation of Islam preached its own brand of salvation for black males. And from the very beginning, the core of the Nation's message has not changed. NOI followers believe that black men can be saved only by being restored as loving leaders in black families where they receive and return adoration and respect. (Alexander 1998, 140)

Dr. Michael Eric Dyson, University Professor of Sociology Georgetown University. Excerpt from The Farrakhan Factor by Amy Alexander

Ron Nixon

No black leader has had more of an impact on the Hip-Hop Generation than Louis Farrakhan. This is increasingly evident in the outward trappings of some young African Americans, the post-Civil Rights Era blacks who came of age after the pitched struggle for integration and who have taken up rap music and black neo-nationalism as their preferred form of cultural expression. Pictures of Farrakhan and the words "Nation of Islam" adorn the postmodern uniforms of black and Latino youth in sparkling suburbs and dying cities alike: On oversized T-shirts, jackets, and clean baseball caps, the silk-screened image of Farrakhan often shares space with those of Marcus Garvey, Malcolm X, and Nelson Mandela. From portable CD players and thumping auto-speakers come the sounds of hip-hop artists, their song lyrics sprinkled with allusions to NOI teachings and tensions between blacks and Jews.

Less conspicuously, black students are the largest consumers of NOI publications, and Farrakhan is undoubtedly the most sought-after speaker on black college campuses. Thousands of black youth joined adults to fill an Atlanta hall in 1992 when the minister came to speak-many more, in fact, than turned out across town at Fulton County Stadium to watch the World Series game that took place the same night...In Farrakhan, many black youths see a symbol of defiance and an alternative to established black leadership.

Some youth use kinship language when speaking of Farrakhan, with words like "brother" and "love" helping them describe their feelings for the minister.

"I love Farrakhan without question or reservation," Jason Broom, a twenty-six year-old African-American in Kansas City, told Newsweek magazine in March 1997. "He's a strong, stand-up black man. I don't practice his religion but I support him. He never turned on us on the street. He's for turning us to men." (Alexander 1998, 184-185)

Ron Nixon is a staff writer at the Roanoke (Virginia) Times. Excerpt from The Farrakhan Factor by Amy Alexander

Robert Michael Franklin

But what is Farrakhan's role in the political realm today? First, he is a prosecuting attorney on behalf of this nation's poor and oppressed minorities. He understands his role to be one of forcefully pointing out discrepancies between American political rhetoric and the reality of black American life. His eloquence and analytic gifts, extraordinary memory, and refined debating skills uniquely qualify him to represent the cause of the unemployable masses which most civil rights organizations and churches have not consistently advanced. Farrakhan speaks to black audiences in a manner that resembles old southern preachers who preach for two or three hours without notes, modulating their presentations between impassioned intensity and humorous, mischievous conversation. One has to sit in his presence to appreciate the quality of his dramatic performance. Many young blacks have been motivated (some would say seduced) by Farrakhan's charisma. Unemployed young people have banded with him, and he has given them hope. Many cannot read or write and are therefore ineligible for the job opportunities which Rev. Jackson and other civil rights leaders generate through protest and bargaining. Farrakhan demonstrates to such young people that after they have been rejected by the wider society they have a chance to become self-respecting persons within their own community.

He has gone into prisons and helped to reform numbers of America's most troublesome population. He has preached family stability and male-female mutual respect in a way that makes him sound more like Jerry Falwell than Malcolm X. But the black underclass has embraced his conservative ethical teachings and his Dale Carnegie-style lessons on personal hygiene, dress, manners, and salesmanship...

Second, Farrakhan is a prosecuting attorney for the Islamic faith and Afro-American Muslims. No other non-Christian leader in black America has so forcefully indicted the Christian tradition for its tacit and explicit racism, classism and hypocrisy, and still managed to command large audiences in the most prestigious churches across the nation. Farrakhan knows the Christian tradition intimately from his years as an altar boy in the Episcopal Church. Indeed, I think that he is drenched with the Anglicanism of his formative years. He believes that all things should be done decently and in order, that religion is a matter of rational understanding and that religious authorities, hierarchy, and traditions should be respected-all motifs which are emphasized in most quarters of the Episcopal community. Farrakhan also reminds us that Islam is not a parochial Arab tradition but a world-wide religion that creates a global community of Muslims who worship Allah. (Franklin 2001)

SalimMuwakkil

He is a remarkably gifted man. With his eloquence, his physical grace, and his flair for the dramatic, he is, by far, Black America's finest orator. His considerable intelligence and organizing abilities combine in a rare synthesis of leadership that has placed him near the top of several black public opinion polls. He's addressed millions of people in the last few years and was the only one capable of pulling off the enormously successful Million Man March. His popularity among African-Americans is even more unlikely. Although the Nation's message is as conservative and as unsensual as that of the most rigid Christian fundamentalist sect, he manages to attract the interest of the most testosterone-saturated segment of African-American community-young men. Listen to some rap records these days, and you're likely to be startled by a stern Farrakhan sermon floating incongruously over a deep bass groove.

Farrakhan seems pretty much unparalleled in his ability to corral the raging energies of this hip-hop generation. One of the ironies of gangsta rap is that pioneering purveyors of the genre also are attracted strongly to Farrakhan's Nation of Islam (many, in fact, are members). The Nation traditionally has attracted the outlaw element among African-Americans. Keep in mind the gangsta pedigree of Malcolm ("Detroit Red") Little who later became Malcolm X. One of the major reasons Farrakhan's group is accorded such street-level respect is its historical connection to the black "underclass."

Although Farrakhan's fiery oratory is heavy with race-man swagger and challenge, he also urges self-discipline, family reverence, ethnic solidarity, hard work, honesty, civility, and all the other virtues held dear by Judeo-Christian civilization. The Nation's rehabilitative success among people utterly forsaken and abandoned by the rest of society recently has prompted mainstream black organizations to look more favorable in Farrakhan's direction. (Alexander 1998, 207)

SalimMuwakkil, Chicago writer and editor of In These Times. He is a former editor of Muhammad Speaks. Excerpt from The Farrakhan Factor by Amy Alexander

Gwendolyn Brooks

Farrakhan. We don't have tea. I have met the Avidly Assaulted One once. About a quarter century ago, a woman poet, then a Muslim, brought him to meet my husband and myself. He was impressively relaxed. He brought no guards, no guns. We were impressed by his warm eyes, his kind patience, flexible dignity. He listened to our ideas. He listened to every word we said. He waited for us to finish our sentences. He never interrupted. (Today, interruption is an Art.) He did not feel the need to pastor. At least, he did not pastor. He did not ask us to join anything. This man I have not seen since. He is, however, a member of the Black Family. He is a Family Picture. I look at the picture. I don't want to forget that this individual has saved a lot of sick-souled, gasping, bare-footed Blacks no one else cared to save. He has fed them, medicated them, detoxicated them, schooled them: thus making many of our lives, homes, and little children a SMIDGEN safer. (Alexander 1998, 270-271)

Gwendolyn Brooks is a Pulitzer Prize winning poet in Chicago. Excerpt from The Farrakhan Factor by Amy Alexander

Professor Derrick Bell

Unlike those conservatives, black and white, who only preach self-help to the poor as a crowd-pleasing abstraction, Farrakhan's formulas emphasize the Nation of Islam's experience in educating black children, rehabilitating black prisoners, ridding black communities of drug dealers, and rebuilding respect for self-the essential prerequisite for individuals determined to maintain the struggle against the racism that burdens our lives and , unless curbed, will destroy this country." (M. L. Farrakhan 1993)

Henry Louis Gates Jr.

Talk story about Minister Louis Farrakhan's sermon at the Million Man March. Henry Louis Gates, Jr., asks five masters of black sacred oratory to give a strictly professional assessment of a colleague's delivery. THE REVEREND WYATT T. WALKER (Canaan Baptist Church, Harlem): Even though I have my quarrels with Louis Farrakhan, I would say that on a scale of ten he was about a twelve, oratorically speaking. THE REVEREND JAMES A. FORBES (Riverside Church, Harlem): As a piece of communication, it was an extraordinary moment. In terms of style, especially in his public condemnation of the President and whites, and so forth, there was a balance of courtesy and critique that I liked. (Gates 1995, 33)

Daniel K. Tabor, City Councilman

The appeal of Farrakhan's POWER (People Organized Working for Economic Rebirth) program for blacks has nothing to do with anti-Semitism. Jews are not the issue; the appeal is in its call for the economic development of the black community, and Farrakhan's program offers sound steps for that development. It should be endorsed and supported by the Urban League, National Association for the Advancement of Colored People, the Black Agenda (a coalition of black organizations working for economic development) and by all black elected officials, not because it is Farrakhan's program but because it will work for us. Black people have tried to be everything to everyone else. It is time for us to be pro-black for ourselves. (Tabor 1985)

Robert A. Jordan

If any speech from last Saturday's Washington march grows in greatness - as did Dr. Martin Luther King Jr.'s of 20 years ago - it will not be the one delivered by Rev. Jesse Jackson. Jackson was expected to be the most inspiring speaker at this year's march because of his oratorical skills and popular appeal among blacks and many whites. As a result, most of the news media, particularly television, focused on Jackson and his final words - "March on. Dream on. March on. Dream on. Our time has come." But as for highlighting the best, most inspiring speaker that day, the media - and television in particular - focused on the wrong man. Although he drew a standing ovation from many of his fans, Jackson was hardly awe-inspiring, and his speech is unlikely to be cast as one of the more memorable of our time. Many marchers felt, perhaps because of high expectations, that his performance was disappointing. One of the best speeches, according to reporters and marchers, was delivered by NAACP Executive Director Benjamin Hooks, who focused his early remarks on politics - "Reagan no more in '84" - and later, assuming his role as a Baptist preacher, ended his speech with the religious fervor that reaches such audiences, as King did so well 20 years ago. However, many who listened to the 40 speakers said the most inspiring speech was given by a lesser-known figure, Louis Farrakhan, organizer of the new Nation of Islam, a Black Muslim religious group. In fact, Farrakhan, who followed Jackson on the speaker's rostrum, was not even mentioned by the news media in the next day's reports. One reason is that they already had their minds made up that Jackson, currently the most popular activist in America, was going to be the focal point for that news event no matter how poorly he performed. Yet it was Farrakhan, one marcher said, who gave him "goose bumps" when he spoke. And it was a black postal worker and a black private business consultant who said that Farrakhan "said some very good things." For example, he told the diverse religious, racial and ethnic groups that "we cannot tolerate any longer these artificial barriers that divide us as a people." Twenty years ago, or even 10, no self-respecting Muslim would have made such a speech. At that time, they were preaching black separatism. But in recent years they have begun to include whites in their membership, and have worked to improve relations with Christian organizations. Farrakhan, whose eloquence has been heard mostly by black Muslims, said in a clear, ringing voice that "this government must say that they will overcome this desire to tell others how to live abroad while neglecting Americans at home." But he added that whether America overcomes this problem or not "we the poor, we the oppressed, we the blacks, we the Hispanics, we the disinherited, we the rejected and the despised, we will overcome and then together we will be able to say in the words of Dr. Martin Luther King - free at last, free at last, thank God Almighty we have united and made freedom a reality at last." Some reporters as well as marchers did not even hear Farrakhan's speech, partly because they left after hearing Jackson, and partly because Farrakhan did not have the name recognition of Jackson, Hooks, or others at the march. His moving speech may not come close in rank to King's great speech. Not many do. But it should not have been ignored. Ironically, King's "I Have A Dream" speech of 20 years ago was almost totally ignored - except in the New York Times - in press accounts the following day. The speech, which King largely ad libbed after he felt the spiritual mood of the crowd, did not become famous until years later. However, perhaps because Farrakhan's Muslim organization does not give him the status of blacks such as King, Jackson or Hooks, his speech may not grow with the passage of time. But it certainly did not deserve to be a victim of the media's pre-occupation with the charismatic Jackson. (Jordan 1983)

Black Entertainment Television

"An overwhelming percentage of our users agreed that Minister Farrakhan made the most positive impact on the Black community over the past year and chose him as the person most worthy to receive the honor of BET.com's 2005 Person of the Year," said Retha Hill, BET.com's vice president for Content.

They agreed that he has done what no other African American leader has: "mobilize hundreds of thousands of Blacks around the issues of atonement and empowerment, and to convince the masses of our people that we must be the primary catalysts and engines for positive change in our communities," she said.

"I am greatly honored and extremely humbled that the BET.com users have chosen me as the 2005 Person of the Year, especially since the nominees for such an honor are some of the greatest members of the Black community in the world; Ms. Oprah Winfrey, Senator Barack Obama, the father of BET Robert L. Johnson and the suffering victims of Hurricane Katrina of New Orleans," Minister Farrakhan told BET.com.

"Honor is never deserved until after the work and mission is completed. The work of the liberation of our people, and the poor and oppressed around the globe is a long, difficult, protracted struggle.

"So, I accept this great honor as encouragement to work as hard as I can in the twilight years of my life to facilitate the success of this ongoing struggle."

Minister Farrakhan said his next move is to continue the work of building the Millions More Movement, which he said will utilize the skill and talent of our people to lift us up.

The minister told BET.com that the Millions More Movement faced many obstacles, but with faith in God, hard work, and the unity of those whose desire it was to create the movement, "we have overcome many obstacles and still are overcoming obstacles in the pathway of our success."

In 1995, Farrakhan became the chief organizer --and a leader -- of a large rally of African-American men in Washington, D.C. Known as the Million Man March, the event was designed to encourage Black men to take personal responsibility for improving conditions in Black America. The crowd was estimated to be up to a million people or more. (Staff 2005)

Wyclef Jean

The reason why I believe it is important for the Honorable Minister Louis Farrakhan to come to Haiti, because the Honorable Minister Louis Farrakhan is one of the most powerful people in the world. I want Haitian people to know their powers. We know that the Honorable Minister Farrakhan has Jamaican roots. In the history we read about Boukman, the Honorable Minister Louis Farrakhan is speaking in the spirit of Boukman. I studied him in the United States. I remember one time when he got all of us in a room, Wyclef, Jay Z and told us guys "the real power it to unite." Today the message I bring to all the Haitian people is that unity produces power. A lot of people when they hear Wyclef speaking, they don't realize I am speaking from the knowledge of my father. The Honorable Minister Louis Farrakhan has been my teacher for a long time. I want to tell you something that is important about this man that is sitting next to me (Minister Farrakhan). I think about 7 to 8 years ago, this man told me about 7 or 8 years ago that I was going to be a presidential candidate and at that time I didn't know what he was talking about. I didn't know I was going to lose (laughter). I want to tell everyone who is listening in to Radio Caraibes, there is no question this wonderful man (Minister Farrakhan) cannot answer, so I thank the listeners of Radio Caraibes for having him here. (FCNN 2011)

Erykah Badu

Louis Farrakhan is a Superhero, that's a beautiful brave being (Badu 2013)

Mary J. Blige

Thank you Minister Farrakhan for spending time with us and sharing your words of wisdom with us. We love you so much (Blige 2013)

Journalist Ellen Hume

Mr. Jackson has disavowed Mr. Farrakhan's words. But he has refused to go further and denounce the man or renounce his political support. The candidate insists that he can't "muzzle" the Muslim leader; Mr. Jackson adds, "Minister Farrakhan has a very high batting average for fighting for good." That view may have cost Mr. Jackson white votes, but it may also have intensified his support in the black community. "We are convinced that the white establishment is trying to divide us," says Lu Palmer, a black political activist in Chicago. "We were concerned how we were going to keep things going for Jackson. The media gave it to us by jumping on Farrakhan." Whatever the case, Mr. Farrakhan -- unknown to the white community a few months ago -- apparently has influence in black America far beyond his estimated 10,000 hard-core religious followers. Moreover, Jackson campaign officials say that Mr. Farrakhan, who has ties to Arab leaders, played a crucial role in Mr. Jackson's success in freeing U.S. flier Robert Goodman from Syria...After replacing Malcolm X as head of the coveted Black Muslim Harlem Temple No. 7, Mr. Farrakhan met Jesse Jackson for the first time in 1972. Mr. Jackson, as a civil-rights leader, called a press conference to support the Muslims after a police incident at the temple. It was a rare moment of friendship between the separatist Muslims and the civil-rights movement they had scorned; Louis Farrakhan never forgot it. "We are not close associates or what one would call buddies. But we mutually admire each other," Mr. Farrakhan says. When he learned that Mr. Jackson was running for president, he broke Muslim tradition and registered to vote, sending a signal that prompted many black nationalists around the country to follow suit and register in order to vote for Mr. Jackson. Thomas N. Todd, a Chicago lawyer who is one of Mr. Jackson's closest associates, says regarding Mr. Jackson's showing so far, "My personal opinion is that we wouldn't have been able to do what we did in Philadelphia, Chicago, New York and the South without Minister Farrakhan." He adds that Mr. Farrakhan was a "substantial part of the success" of Mr. Jackson's Syria mission to free Lt. Goodman, although he got little publicity at the time. "To assume Minister Farrakhan is on some lunatic fringe, away from the mainstream, is not true," Mr. Todd emphasizes. "His influence extends far beyond the Nation of Islam, to black professionals, educators and others who agree with Farrakhan's position on some of the social ills and how we got there." Mr. Farrakhan's following isn't nearly as large as the Jackson support in black Christian churches, others stress. "There's no comparison," says the Rev. Charles Stith, a black Methodist minister in Boston. "You're comparing apples and peanuts." Yet it was Mr. Farrakhan's highly disciplined followers who helped the Jackson campaign get off the ground. They were the candidate's original bodyguards before the U.S. Secret Service stepped in; they contribute money collected in baskets at their religious meetings and they continue to stage the huge Jackson rallies in key cities like Philadelphia, New York and Chicago. Mr. Farrakhan is a "leader, like Benjamin Hooks, John Jacob, Vernon Jordan and the others," concludes Dorothy Leavell, the publisher of the New Crusader, a black newspaper in Chicago. (Mr. Hooks is the executive director of the National Association for the Advancement of Colored People, Mr. Jacobs is the president of the national Urban League and Mr. Jordan is a former president of that group.) At another time and place, Mr. Jackson and Mr. Farrakhan might have been rivals. "He is probably the only other person, in terms of charisma, who could challenge Jesse," says Boston's Mr. Stith. "He's powerful. (Hume 1984)

Harry L. Thomas, Sr.

On Oct. 24, I did indeed present a resolution to Minister Louis Farrakhan. In its introductory clause, that resolution reads: "To recognize the Nation of Islam for their commitment and dedication to the 'War on Drugs.' "As that clause states, the Nation of Islam was honored for its fight against drugs. The resolution addressed not what Mr. Farrakhan stands for or has said, but what he, as leader of the Nation of Islam, has done. While others talked about a solution to the drug activity in Mayfair Mansions, the Nation of Islam acted and achieved outstanding success in the face of ostensibly insurmountable odds. The resolution praises the Nation for their "commitment and dedication," no more, no less. Should I, or the D.C. Council, be condemned or second-guessed for acknowledging the success of the Nation for recapturing our neighborhoods from the drug dealers? The article also observed that, because of Minister Farrakhan's "racially inflammatory remarks ... black politicians are uncertain whether to openly support him or openly denounce him." I cannot speak for other black politicians, but as for Harry Thomas, I unequivocally support the minister and the Nation of Islam for their efforts to stem the tide of drugs in our neighborhoods. My feelings in this regard are so unflinching that I would, for once, even give unequivocal support to The Washington Post should it decide to man the front lines in the fight against drugs. In that instance, to say that my "unequivocal support" for The Post for its drug-fighting efforts translates into my support of The Post in general would be a gross misstatement of fact. Further, if The Post undertook such a drug-fighting effort, but does not represent my views in general, are my only two choices to "openly support" it or "openly denounce" it? Finally, my support of the Nation of Islam and its leader, Minister Farrakhan, will continue for as long as their effective leadership in helping rid the black community of the scourge of drugs continues. That support, however, will extend to any others who choose to assist in that fight. (ThomasJr. 1989)

William Raspberry

Farrakhan says what so many black people believe but have learned not to say in public: for instance, that Jews wield tremendous influence in the news and entertainment media. That doesn't mean that most blacks accept Farrakhan's notion of a small Jewish cabal that meets in Hollywood or in a Park Avenue apartment to decide which ideas and trends are to be foisted off on the public. But few of us doubt the disproportionate influence of Jews-for good or ill- on what we see on television or in the movies. Nor do blacks doubt the disproportionate influence of Jews on American foreign policy, particularly with regard to political and economic support of Israel. But we also know that to say these things is to be accused of anti-Semitism. That's why blacks can cheer when Farrakhan says them, even in gross overstatement. (Raspberry 1990)

Nathan McCall

I suspect that, for some white Americans, complaints about Farrakhan are a smoke screen to conceal their blanket contempt for any black man who attempts to lift us up. White America may now pledge allegiance to the memory of Martin Luther King but black America has not forgotten that King, who preached love, peace and every other noble virtue that we claim to embrace, was intensely disliked and opposed by many whites when he was alive. His plan for a march on Washington 32 years ago was also described as divisive, unnecessary, potentially violent. I have even less patience with so-called black church and political leaders nationwide who have criticized the Million Man March. With all that black men have been going through in recent years, there's been no broad-scale effort -- symbolic or otherwise -- by national black politicians and clergy to inspire us. If there were more black leaders out there with courage and imagination, we'd have done something like this long ago. Everywhere I've gone in recent months, from barber shops in Prince George's County, to college campuses in Kentucky, the irrelevance of this traditional leadership has been clear. Black men -- the regular brothers whose voices are seldom captured on TV or in print -- say they don't need to consult so-called black leaders to determine whether or not to attend the march. (McCall 1995)

Clifton E. Marsh

Minister Louis Farrakhan was one of Jackson's early supporters in running for the presidency. Early in 1983 Minister Louis Farrakhan "wrote Jackson a letter urging him to seek the country's top office and offering his support." Prior to Rev. Jackson being considered a serious candidate, he received no Secret Service protection. Minister Louis Farrakhan directed his "Fruit of Islam" to protect Rev. Jackson on the campaign trail. In each city in which Jackson arrived to speak, he was greeted, escorted, and protected by disciplined cadres of bow tie-wearing black men. When candidate Jackson was finally given Secret Service protection by the U.S. government, the agents would complain that they "couldn't get close to him for the crowd of Muslims around him."

Minister Louis Farrakhan played a significant and vital role in enabling Jesse Jackson to secure the release of navy Lt. Robert Goodman. Minister Louis Farrakhan accompanied Rev. Jackson to Syria. Surely, this would be a test for the ideas of the Honorable Elijah Muhammad. The so-called contrast between Orthodox Islam and the Nation of Islam could derail negotiations, put Lieutenant Goodman's life in further danger, and embarrass the United States and the entire African American community. The charismatic Minister Louis Farrakhan impressed Syria's heads of state, Imams, Muslim scholars, and true believers with his knowledge with his knowledge of Islam and ability to speak perfect Arabic. He led the Jumuah prayer service with all the grace and eloquence of Bilal himself. So much for those who said the international community of Islam would not accept the ideology of the Lost-Found Nation of Islam in America. (Marsh 2000)

Dr. Boyce Watkins

"Minister Farrakhan fascinates many Black people because he represents a type of freedom and truth that they can only dream about. Even those who disavow him in public rely on him behind closed doors because he has the courage and capacity to confront obstacles that leave most Black Americans in fear. He doesn't bend, fold or change his tune due to corporate or political pressure, and he doesn't spend his time tap dancing for White people. He also has a degree of ownership of his own being that is nothing short of extraordinary. The truth is that he has negotiated a relationship with White America in which they may not love him, but they do fear him and respect him. It is mutual respect from White America that Black people are lacking today, largely due to our inability to secure economic, psychological and social self-sufficiency. We get these things from Minister Louis Farrakhan. When I met Minister Farrakhan, I felt like I was talking to my own father. As a Black man who has worked to teach myself to be strong and free, it's difficult to find older Black men who understand my path and journey and can show me how to pursue that path more effectively. My three hours with the Minister in private conversation, my meetings with him in Arizona and our event in Chicago were all life-changing for me and in each case; I knew I had the rare opportunity to be a part of history." (S. Muhammad 2013)

Alabama State Senator Hank Sanders

(The following letter is Senator Sanders response to complaints by the Birmingham Jewish Federation over the appearance of Minister Farrakhan in the state of Alabama, specifically to lend his support influence and popularity to the civil rights leaders' efforts to maintain the right to vote for Black people in the state of Alabama)

Dear Mr. Friedman,

Thank you for your letter expressing concerns about Minister Louis Farrakhan's coming to Alabama to stand with us in fighting to save our voting rights in general and Section 5 in particular. I respond in this open letter because of the extensive communications around this issue.

We are fighting for a basic constitutional right -- the right to vote. It is the right that protects all other rights. The right to vote is so important to us, our children and our children's children. I personally know the terrible sting of not being able to vote. It affects every part of our being, including our sense of worth. The right to vote is extremely critical.

Minister Louis Farrakhan is coming to Alabama at our invitation. We welcome everyone who will stand with us to protect this basic right -- the right to vote, which is under great attack.

You and other Jewish people have and have had the right to vote. It is not under attack. You have not suffered the loss of the right to vote provided by Fifteenth Amendment to U.S. Constitution as we have. You were not prevented from voting for nearly 100 years as our people were. It is a terrible thing that I hope Jewish Americans never have to suffer.

We are fighting to protect a constitutional right -- the right to vote. You are fighting to keep a person out of Alabama because of his exercising his constitutional right to freedom of speech. The words you attribute to him are offensive, but it is his constitutional right to speak. (Additionally, he has denied many of the allegations.) I do not fault you for objecting to offensive language.

You have not publicly stood with us once to protect our constitutional right to vote during the series of events we have held in Alabama, Washington DC and throughout the Southeast, events that commenced in February and continue today. Now you ask us to reject someone who believes in our fight for the constitutional right to vote and is coming to stand side by side and fight. This does not make sense to me.

When US Supreme Court Justice Antonin Scalia made disparaging remarks about Section 5, calling it a "racial preferment" and comparing racial minorities to "child abusers," I did not hear you standing against these racist remarks.

We cannot fault you for whomever you stand with or have stand with you in your struggle. By the same token, we cannot allow you to determine who stands with us in our struggle.

All of us fall short. I know I fall short all the time. While Minister Farrakhan has said things that are offensive (many of which he has denied), he has also lifted many from societal degradation. Should that not count for something? Should we not value people for what they do as well as what they say? I applaud him for the good things he has done.

Finally, if all the people in Alabama who have uttered racist words were removed from Alabama, we would have a greatly depopulated state. I think the same standards ought to apply to all of us, including Minister Louis Farrakhan.

Again, I appreciate your expressing your concerns to me, but the right to vote is too important not to fight for it with all available resources. Please consider this letter in the spirit in which it is intended -- one of forgiveness and inclusion.

Sincerely, Hank Sanders (Sanders 2013)

Tuskegee Alabama Mayor Johnny Ford

"I'm here to say that not only is he(Minister Farrakhan) welcome, with the power invested in me by the people of Tuskegee, Alabama, I hereby proclaim this night as 'Minister Louis Farrakhan Night' in the City of Tuskegee. Not only do I present to him the key to the City of Tuskegee, I'm proud to say that he is honorary mayor of Tuskegee for life!" (A. Muhammad, Farrakhan tells students: You are chosen to build a world! 2013)

National Review

To a great extent, in other words, Farrakhan now *is* the black leadership—the cutting edge, the storm center, the presence against which others are measured. 1985. (National Review 1985)

Frank Paul Jones

Before I discuss Minister **Farrakhan's** speech, I'm gon'na describe what I witnessed. I went there with an idea that Minister **Farrakhan** was an egocentric preacher of hatred. (This is how white media influenced me.) I was wrong. What I witnessed was a very humble man, who has been character assassinated by white media, for speaking the truth as he understood it, and at the time expressed himself as he felt it was necessary.
I witnessed a man who is apprehensive, yet he is willing to risk death for the sake of truth. As he stood inside a bullet-proof case, he cried out to all people including white society and Jews, for help. In that moment, in my eyes, he was not a man of hate, but a man of love; a man of God. He became the unspoken voice for tens of thousands of Black people, holding hands in prayer, who were referring to each other as "my brother" and "my sister" and it was an event full of love. (F. P. Jones 1996)

Prof. Andre C. Willis

The best of the legacy of Farrakhan is twofold. First, he has demonstrated a deep understanding of and shown an unswerving courage to publicly detail the lived reality of anti-black racism. There is simply no Black person in the world that has — over so many years — been as consistent, as unrestricted, and as forthright in defending the humanity of Black people throughout the world against its attackers. This is partially due to the power of black institutions: Minister Farrakhan does not rely on white financial support. It is also due to a sense of discipline and commitment inscribed in his practice as a man of faith. Demonized by some and ostracized by many, Farrakhan's story has been one of "staying the course" for racial uplift.

Second, Farrakhan's captivating speaking style and scriptural knowledge have made him, undoubtedly, one of the great religious orators of our time. His entrancing public speeches, which never lose track of race, are crafted at the intersection of the religious and the political. Farrakhan, in the style of the eighteenth century "Great Awakening" speakers, unapologetically deploys the sacred texts of Christianity and Islam in his public witness. Yet these "religious" speeches are deeply politicized and they rely on different religious traditions. Thus, they stand in a class all by themselves. Further, his visual appeal, stylized voice and phrasing, as well as his effective use of silence are incomparable. When Biblical and Qur'anic scholars begin to attend to the body of his work, this aspect of his legacy will stand even taller. (Willis 2012)

President Ibrahim B. Syed, Ph. D.,

I asked Sheikh Ahmed Tijani as to how he came to know about me. He did not answer me specifically. Later on I came to know a mutual friend recommended my name. I accepted the invitation to attend and speak in several sessions, such as the two plenary sessions on "The Oneness of Allah and the Oneness of His Community", and two workshops on "Islamic Science and Technology", "Islamic Health", and one workshop on "Modern Methods of Propagation for the New Century" and I was assigned the job of a Moderator on a session on "Islamic Science, Technology and Communication Systems for the New Century." Other interesting and timely workshops that were conducted were "The Need to Return to Moral Excellence", "Islamic Education in the New Century", "Islamic Family Life. Courtship and Preparation for Marriage. Strengthening Family and Home Life", "Islamic Law in the New Century", "Islamic Economics and Banking in the New Century", "Conflict Resolution Among Muslims", "The Role of Women in Islam", "The Place of Architecture, Art, and Culture in Islam", "Advancement of Muslims Socially, Politically, and Economically in Western Society, and in other Countries" and Plenary Sessions on "Inter-Faith Dialogue." I accepted the invitation for two reasons, one to share my humble knowledge and secondly to observe first-hand the activities of the controversial organization "The Nation of Islam."

This International Islamic Conference is one of the best I have ever attended in North America or anywhere in the world. It was well organized and executed. Many scholars came from many parts of the world, such as Canada, Mexico, Panama, Trinidad, Sri Lanka, Great Britain, Philippines, Dagestan (Russia), South Africa, Nigeria, Morocco, Gambia, Uganda, Senegal, Ghana, Greek Cyprus, Egypt, Jordon, Palestine, Lebanon, Yemen, United Arab Emirates, and of course from many cities in USA.

The attenders were kept busy from morning till late in the night. I attended the Jumuah prayers at the Mosque Maryam, where we also prayed Maghrib and Isha prayers. The Zuhr and Asr prayers were conducted at the Hilton Inn and Towers. I saw the Hon. Minister Louis Farrakhan praying with us like an Orthodox Muslim or mainstream Muslim. The Muslims in the Community of the Nation of Islam both men and women behaved extremely well and were well dressed. I was impressed with them, as they are a good role model for other Muslims.

The Nation of Islam identifies itself as Islamic. Members call God "Allah," they call themselves Muslims, they teach and worship in mosques, they appeal to the prophet Muhammad (peace be upon him), they recite the Muslim creed, and they view the Qur'an as inspired Scripture. The chief leaders of the NOI (Elijah Muhammad, Malcolm X, and Minister Farrakhan) have all made pilgrimages to Mecca, and at the present time NOI members are instructed to fast during the Muslim month of Ramadan and to consult the *hadith* or traditions ascribed to Prophet Muhammad (pbuh) to determine proper conduct and doctrine. Thus, for broad purposes of classification, it seems reasonable to place the NOI somewhere within the Islamic camp.

I did not witness any controversial thing during my five days of association with them. The final session ended at the McCormick Place where Col. Muammar Qaddafi, the Libyan Leader spoke to the participants by satellite T.V. Also this session was televised all over the Muslim World. The finale of the International Conference was when Imam Farrakhan spoke to the audience for almost two years with his remarkable ability to spellbind and charm the audience. At the end of the session Mr. Jerry Thomas of the Chicago Tribune interviewed me, as others appeared to be reluctant to the interview. In my interview with reference to the Nation of Islam, I told what I witnessed .... "They were first identified as black Muslims. That barrier has been removed. They are now just Muslims, like any other Muslims in the world."

On that final day evening, I received a dinner invitation at the home (Palace or official residence) of the Leader of the Nation of Islam along with all the foreign delegates and a few American delegates. Imam Farrakhan was a gracious host and everyone enjoyed the delicious dishes and a sumptuous dinner. That memorable night was concluded with an individual photo session with the Imam or the Leader of the Nation of Islam...

Muslims who still have doubts and upset should have a dialogue with the Nation of Islam. Alhamdulillah, Muslims are doing very well in Inter-Faith dialogues with Christians and Jews. Why not we have dialogues with the Nation of Islam? I personally believe we must interact with the Nation of Islam with Hikmah (wisdom) and Sabr (patience) in the model of our Rasoolallah (SAS). I completely agree with the sentiments expressed by the popular and well-known Muslim journalist, Mom "Moon" Khan, that "it is time for healing, a time for moving ahead, understanding each other and respecting each other. It is not the time of dividing people and isolating people in a community and putting other communities ahead of each other."...

Muslims of North America will derive immense benefits and rewards by uniting with the Nation of Islam and by welcoming them as our brothers and sisters in Islam. It is highly gratifying to know that the Nation of Islam and the Ministry of Imam Wartih Deen Mohammed have united to advance the cause of Islam and the Muslims in North America. May Allah (SWT) guide us and show us the right path and bring us from darkness unto light. Ameen! (Syed n.d.)

International Islamic Conference

Imam Ahmed Rufai: "As Salaam Alaikum, Brothers and Sisters.

On behalf of the Muslim World, we have the Grand Sheikh of Cypress, Sheikh Muhammad Sobhi Bello; The Grand Sheik of Egypt and Vice President of Al-Azhar University, Sheikh Abu Al Azayem; and The Grand Sheikh of Yemin Sheikh Abu Ghazela and our Sheikh of Ghana and Nigeria Sheikh Abdul Razzaq Tahir Muhyideen, and Sheikh Yusuf Shibly who want to show their admiration for the leadership of our brother The Honorable Minister Louis Farrakhan by recognizing him as an Imam of the Muslim World.

Translator for Sheikh Mohammed Sobhi Bello of Cyprus: "In the Name of Allah (swt), the Most Merciful, the Most Beneficent, blessed are you and blessed is this conference. In the symbol of the leadership and the knowledge of the Qur'an, we signify that, symbolize that by putting this cap on the head of our leader, Brother Louis Farrakhan because the scholars and the knowledgeable are the people who are the inheritors of the Prophets of Allah (swt). And to signify that we have put that on his head in order to show our appreciation and to show that he is knowledgeable and will lead the Islamic Nation, inshallah, with his inspiration." (H. M. Farrakhan 1997)

Professor Mattias Gardell

His long lectures are composed much like orchestral numbers. He starts by displaying a theme, and then varies the expressions, moving his audience to tears and laughter, serious consideration and explosive anger, before reaching the grand finale in which he dramatically drives his points through. Farrakhan combines a number of diverse roles during each sermon, such as the strong warrior, the trickster, the stern father, the heart warmer, the stand-up comedian, the encyclopedic scholar and the Doomsday prophet. As is common in the black church, a kind of dialogue is established as the preaching evokes responses from the audience, with the worshipers shouting cries of approval such as "That's right," "Tell it like it is," "Go on, Minister, go on," and "Teach, Brother teach."
There is no doubt that Farrakhan's oratorical brilliance contributes heavily to his rising popularity and explains, in part, the crowds that jam auditoriums when he speaks. Farrakhan is able to attract larger audiences than any other black spokesperson: 35,000 people showed up at Madison Square Garden,

New York; 17,000 in Los Angeles; 26,000 in Detroit; 19,000 and then 15,000 in Atlanta; 15,000 in Chicago; 21,000 at Jacob Javits Center in New York, and 10,000 in Baltimore. (Gardell 1996)
–*Mattias Gardell, Professor of Theology Uppsala University, Sweden; In The Name of Elijah Muhammad, Louis Farrakhan and The Nation of Islam*

Socialist Economist and Professor Dr. Michael D. Yates

Cedric Muhammad: Earlier this year you met with the Honorable Minister Louis Farrakhan and were presented with an introduction to the Economic Blueprint of the Honorable Elijah Muhammad. What were your impressions of both the Minister and that Program?

Michael D. Yates, PhD.: I was impressed with Minister Farrakhan's energy and considerable knowledge about the many economic issues we discussed. His concern and love for those in need was evident. Minister Farrakhan also proved a gracious and generous host in his home, where we enjoyed a fine meal and good conversation. He and his family went out of their way to make everyone feel welcome. It was certainly a day to remember and reflect upon.

In terms of the Economic Blueprint, I found it worth developing further. Much of it is applicable today. Its most fundamental principle is that we must control resources if we are to address our economic and social difficulties. And we must be part of a project larger than ourselves, one motivated by ideals of human solidarity and not just by self-interest.

Concretely, the Blueprint asks us to stop spending money foolishly and to save for both future growth and emergencies. This seems like excellent advice in a society built upon mindless consumption. Next, the Blueprint wants our savings to be pooled for community investment, in what we might call a development bank. Large sums of money could be raised from the small savings of millions of people. Then the bank could use the funds to benefit the community. Land could be purchased and agricultural enterprises begun. Distribution mechanisms could be established to get the food into the homes of those in need, and stores could be set up for food sales.

The Blueprint has been partially realized, first by the Honorable Elijah Muhammad and then by Minister Farrakhan, notably through the purchase of farmland and the growing of organic food. At our meeting, we discussed the possibility of building on this. Perhaps cooperative businesses could be started, such as urban farming and housing, both of which could include the training of those in need of meaningful work.

Minister Farrakhan made an important point. Although the blueprint focused on community self-help, the larger society, as embodied in the government, owed something to the people who built the nation. So, we must demand that our national government ensure the economic security of its people. As the Nation of Islam's ten-point platform of 1963 demanded (and that of the original Black Panther Party reiterated), we must insist on full employment, decent housing, good education, an end to police brutality in our communities, an end to an unjust criminal justice system, and access to land, housing, clothing, and justice. (C. Muhammad 2013)

Dr. Michael D. Yates, an expert on labor and economics and the Associate Editor of Monthly Review (http://monthlyreview.org) one of the most influential Socialist publications in the world. In addition to providing instruction at the University of Pittsburgh, Johnstown, MDY has taught working people for many years throughout America.

Holy People of The World: A Cross-Cultural Encyclopedia (Misbahudeen Ahmed Rufai)

Louis Farrakhan follows in the footsteps of Elijah Muhammad, leader of the Nation of Islam (NOI) from 1934 to 1975, to whom he refers as the "man who taught me what I know" (Haskins 1996). Born Louis Eugene Walcott on May 11, 1933, in Roxbury, Massachusetts, Minister Farrakhan and his late brother, Alvin, were raised by his mother, a native of Saint Kitts. He never knew his father, a Jamaican native.

To his followers, Farrakhan is God's instrument for a "New World Order of Peace and Righteousness on the foundation of Truth and Justice; to put down tyrants and to change the world into a Heaven on Earth" (ibid.). Elijah Muhammad is the Moses, while Farrakhan is the Aaron who will lead black America to the Promised Land. His ministers often introduce him as "our divine leader and guide." In 1997, Muslim scholars and spiritual leaders from

Africa, Asia, Australia, the Middle East, and the Americas, converging in Chicago, turbaned and acknowledged him as an imam of the Muslim world. Farrakhan's mission is expressed by the title of the Nation of Islam's official newspaper, *The Final Call*. The paper's logo is a trumpet, which signifies the end of time and the beginning of God's judgment. This mission is best articulated in *Farrakhan, The Traveler*, one of the longest-running columns since the paper's inception in 1979. The columnist, Jabril Muhammad, describes Farrakhan as the fulfillment of Jesus' predictions of the signs of the end of this world and of his return, hailing him as the long-awaited *Mahdi* (messiah) of Islam. In 1993, Minister Farrakhan published his first book, *A Torchlight for America*, to provide a guide to the nation's spiritual abyss. (Jestice 2004)

Time Magazine

In a historic cover for Time Magazine's February 28, 1994 edition, Time did a survey of Black America's view of Minister Farrakhan. They found that 73% of Black people were familiar with The Minister and that 66.7% held a favorable view of him. The survey was conducted via a telephone poll. Poll respondents were asked several questions about Minister Farrakhan and the following results were compiled.

Someone who says things the country should hear.......... 70%

An effective leader......................67%

Speaks the truth 63%

Good for the black community.......62%

A role model for black youth.........53%

Someone you personally admire 40%

A bigot and a racist....................34%

(Asked of 364 African Americans familiar with Farrakhan. Sampling error is plus or minus 5%.) (Henry III, et al. 1994)

President Nelson Mandela

Our meeting was able to cover those things that we considered to be fundamental. And there was no issue that arose on which there was disagreement. He has explained his position. His view are identical with the principles that I put forward. (The Final Call 1996)

USA Today

One year after the Million Man March turned the Mall in Washington, D.C., into a flowing sea of black humanity, one year after the marchers returned home with high hopes and renewed energy, the question remains: Was there a lasting effect?

Was the march called by Nation of Islam leader Louis Farrakhan only a fleeting, goose bump-raising moment for black Americans? Or was it the beginning of a lasting national movement, like the one that grew out of Martin Luther King's 1963 March on Washington? Will the Million Man March one day be viewed as such a pivotal event that people who weren't there will say they were?

Interviews with dozens of marchers suggest that many of the men who marched on Oct. 16, 1995, took to heart the messages of black self-reliance and responsibility, and that they channeled those messages into action.

Men like Jacob Wheeler III, of Los Angeles, who went home and started Summit 2000. The coalition of 16 organizations had the goal of helping 1 million more black families across the country own their own homes.

Wheeler left the March feeling as if "it was all kind of a dream." But, he says, "By the end of January we decided this was a dream that could become reality."

And reality, he says, can be measured. …

- Up to 15,000 new applicants wanting to adopt black children.

Leonard Dunston, president of the National Association of Black Social Workers, says his group was flooded with 2,500 phone calls just two hours after its toll-free number was announced at the march. Another 12,500 inquiries have come in since. Dunston says more than 300 children have found homes as a direct result of the Million Man March.

But with more than 40,000 black children available for adoption, "it's still a drop in the bucket," says Maureen Hogan, national executive director of Adopt A Special Kid/America, a private adoption agency....

- Increased interest among black men in serving their communities.

Anecdotal evidence suggests this may be the march's most tangible legacy.

In Philadelphia, 19 men joined the Big Brother program during a November 1995 recruiting drive as a direct result of the march.

"Many of them were still on that high of 'you got to do something for the community,' " says Cheryl Dennis, head of recruitment for the Big Brother/

Big Sister Association of Philadelphia.

The Memphis Big Brother organization estimates that 33 of the 100 people picked up in last year's recruitment drive came as a direct result of the march.

In Denver, 100 black men went door-to-door in a neighborhood after a 3-year-old was killed in a drive-by shooting, seeking information. In a neighborhood not known for cooperating with police, their efforts helped lead to an arrest.

In Atlanta, the local organizing committee held a drive to encourage people to open accounts at black-owned banks. Timothy McDonald, leader of the committee, said the drive resulted in $3 million being transferred into Atlanta's black-owned banks. The committee also ran a Saturday school during the summer that helped 75 students with reading, writing, math, geography and English literature.

Although assessing the success of the Million Man March on a national level yields no clear answers, it is clear that something did happen.

At the very least, black men had one sun-drenched day to shine and show the best of themselves. And the communities from which they came had hope that problems that had besieged them for decades might finally be addressed.

The memory of thousands of positive black men gathered in Washington is so powerful that it still overwhelms Masai Minters, 45, director of student supports services at the University of California Los Angeles.

"It was a winning day for those men who have experienced a lot of losing days," Minters says.

"I still feel it today." (Fields and Puente 1996)

Journalist Vince Beiser

Whatever else, Louis Farrakhan may be, let no one say he is not a gracious host – even to a Jewish journalist. Before beginning our interview at his palatial residence in an affluent, integrated South Chicago neighborhood, the leader of the Nation of Islam makes sure that my photographer and I are comfortable in our high-backed chairs at his long dining-room table, well supplied with pineapple juice and coffee, and apologizes for having made us wait, even though we actually arrived early. The house feels peaceful, the quiet disturbed only occasionally by the muffled crackles of the walkie-talkies carried by the neatly dressed security men passing by outside. Soft light flows in from a skylight over the adjacent atrium, in the center of which a fountain surrounded by lush green plants burbles serenely. The carpets are deep and soft, the floors marble, the chandeliers crystal. The mosque-like mansion is home to Farrakhan, 64, and is also the NOI's symbolic headquarters - their black equivalent of the White House, he has called it.

"I want you to feel at home, and ask any questions you feel your readers would be interested in," says Farrakhan, his voice as honey-smooth as a

Motown Singer. One reason he has become perhaps the nation's most important African-American leader is immediately obvious: The man practically glows with charisma and charm. The Honorable Minister is dressed casually today, having swapped his usual dark suit and bow tie for an off-white pants and tunic ensemble set off by a couple of hefty gold rings and a gold necklace. Farrakhan, who always has so much to say about Jews, has agreed to speak to them directly through an interview with a Jewish publication, one of only a handful of times he has done so and the first since the Million Man March he convened in Washington in 1995 catapulted him to the forefront of black political leadership. (Beiser 1997)

Julius Lester

The appearance of Louis Farrakhan at Madison Square Garden on October 7 demonstrated, without doubt that he is now America's preeminent black leader. Benjamin Hooks of the NAACP could not have filled the Garden. There would not have been people standing against the walls on every level of the arena to hear John Jacob of the National Urban League. Jesse Jackson might just have filled the Garden. But Farrakhan filled not only the 20,000-plus seats; he also drew another 3,000 to 5,000 people to watch the whole event on closed circuit television in the Felt Forum next door.

If people get the leader they deserve, then something dire has happened in Black America. No people should make the journey from Martin Luther King Jr. to Louis Farrakhan in fewer than 20 years. Most of these were not members of Farrakhan's Nation of Islam, and never will be. Nonetheless, they came there to applaud, cheer, yell, and shout. What they came to voice approval of was apparent from the start. (Lester 1985)

TUSKEGEE-MACON COUNTY NAACP BRANCH

PO Box 618
Tuskegee Institute, AL 36087

~Unanimously Adopted Resolution~

"In Support of Tuskegee University
(Administration, Staff & Students)
And
Endorsement of Invitation
To
Honorable Minister Louis Farrakhan"

WHEREAS, In 1881, over 131 years ago, Tuskegee (Institute) University was founded by Dr. Booker T. Washington. It has thrived and survived as one of the top rated Historically Black Colleges/Universities (HBCU) in the country; and

WHEREAS, Tuskegee University (TU) has also become one of the nation's most outstanding institutions in the Academy of Higher Education; and

WHEREAS, The mission and goals of the Institution have been sustained, developed, and advanced by its progressive leadership of six (6) Presidents; and

Resolution, continued   -2-

WHEREAS, Throughout its history, speakers of renowned statue and leadership positions have graced the campus with messages of spiritual, intellectual, social and political magnitude and persuasion; and

WHEREAS, Both the academic climate and exposure opportunities for the enrolled students prepare them to be investigative and responsive to a speaker's message with an open mind of intellectual discernment; and

WHEREAS, Dr. Gilbert L. Rochon, currently serving as President of Tuskegee University, has vowed to "Bring the World to Tuskegee and Tuskegee to the World;" and

WHEREAS, Recently, an invitation was extended to Minister Louis Farrakhan to visit and speak at Tuskegee. His visit would be part of an ongoing series of addresses at HBCU campuses. This invitation, initiated by the Tuskegee University Muslim Student Association and the Black Belt Deliberative Dialogue Group, was sanctioned and endorsed by the Administration of the University; and

WHEREAS, Concern has been expressed in the press, by a member of the TU Board of Trustees, regarding Minister Farrakhan's visit, scheduled for March 21-22, 2013. It is especially disheartening that the Board Member stated: "We shouldn't endorse him anymore than we endorse the Ku Klux Klan. They are two organizations of a similar breed;" and

WHEREAS, TU Alumni across the country are concerned about the negative news blast that the Trustee has

Resolution, continued   -3-

interjected into this scheduled visit on the campus of Alma Mater.

NOW, THEREFORE, BE IT RESOLVED, That the Tuskegee-Macon County NAACP Branch, an active affiliate of the Oldest Civil Rights Organization in the Nation, recognizes and supports diversity and cross-cultural exposure for the TU Family, particularly its students.

BE IT FURTHER RESOLVED, That the NAACP Branch commends the groups for their vision when extending an invitation to Honorable Minister Louis Farrakhan. We urge the community to support the visit with our presence and participation in the sessions.

BE IT FURTHER RESOLVED, That Tuskegee-Macon County NAACP Branch welcomes Minister Farrakhan upon this, a return visit to Tuskegee (Institute) University. He is the Father of a proud Tuskegee Graduate. He is also a former speaker at the University.
We further endorse the recent letter of support that was transmitted by the Black Belt Deliberative Dialogue Group to the President of Tuskegee University

FINALLY, BE IT RESOLVED, That the NAACP Branch shall deliver a copy of this Resolution to the Tuskegee University Board of Trustees, seeking the Board's support for the visit of Minister Farrakhan. A copy shall also be delivered to: Tuskegee University-Office of the President; The Student Government Association of TU; The Tuskegee National Alumni Association-Board of Directors; The Press; Alabama State Conference of NAACP; and the

Resolution, continued   -4-

National Office of NAACP, Benjamin Todd Jealous, President/CEO.

Unanimously Adopted On This Date:

<u>*March 19, 2013*</u>

<u>*Barbara Howard*</u>
Barbara Howard
NAACP Branch President

<u>*Elaine C. Harrington*</u>
Dr. Elaine C. Harrington
NAACP Branch Program Coordinator
&
Drafter of Resolution

****
***
*

This impressive list of laudatory comments regarding Minister Farrakhan's value is extremely compelling. It is a witness bearer to his function as an instrument that Allah (God) is using to reach the masses with the truth. These are testimonies from government officials, Black people, White people, professionals, entertainers, spiritual teachers, politicians, leaders, journalists and more. We therefore conclude that Minister Farrakhan is unique, peerless, extraordinary and divine

A Portrait in Humility: What Does Minister Farrakhan Think About Himself?

(The following are excerpts from the book Closing The Gap: Inner Views with The Honorable Minister Louis Farrakhan by Jabril Muhammad page 70-72)

"I was telling Brother Jabril [two nights earlier] that no matter what people say of me and how people are saying things all over the world, I feel like a little boy inside of a mature man. Now look at that picture: a little boy inside of a mature man. As the man is getting older and wiser, the people outside are relating to this mature man who is representing Allah(God), the Honorable Elijah Muhammad, Prophet Muhammad and the Truth, but, on the inside is this little boy who is almost oblivious to the kudos and the praise and all that is being said to the mature man on the outside. The little fellow on the inside may want to play. He may want to do somelittle silly thing. He is not even aware of the greatness that Allah (God) is making of him. He is just happy being a little boy on the inside of this mature man.

I keep thinking, as I look at myself, no matter what people say, "how great he is, yet I see myself jus like I was when we (looking at his wife) were back in Roxbury, Massachusetts and I am this little fellow respectful of my elders and always willing to do little things to help this one and that one; never taking myself seriously. That is my protection. The little boy on the inside is protected from all of the praise and the kudos, fame, popularity, adulation, and acclamation, on the mature man growing on the outside.

The little fellow, if there is a carton that could be drawn of a man growing in stature and the lines in his face and the wisdom that he speaks and the audiences cheering, and on the inside there is this little boy playing hopscotch or playing with his marbles and he is oblivious to the people outside saying great and wondeful things about him. He is hitting that marble. He isjust doing his "little boy" things.

So, no matter what people say; no matter how much they praise me; it does not affect me, because it only reaches the head of the old man, but the little fellow on the inside didn't hear it. He doesn't know it. You know? I don't know why I made that picture; but that's the way I feel inside.

Even though I know these words that you [Jabril] write are true and I know I am the representative of this Messianic dispensation; I know that I am that. I know that. I know that. But, then, I don't know it. Do you know what I mean? I know that I am becoming a very great man. But I am not aware to the point where I am carried away with myself, because the little boy on the inside does not allow it.

You know how old people can sit at a table and talk and the little boy is looking for a way to get away from table so he can do "little boy" things? Am I making sense? [We all laugh; for he is crystal clear and in a very touching and sensitive manner.] That's a heck of a picture, isn't it?

So I don't know what games people have on their minds, but little children do ot [arrogantly] judge people. Little children have a way of looking at people, they may not go to everybody, but they are innocent. And because they are innocent, they have to be protected. That's that little fellow within. Now, the old guy might be wise enough to protect the little fellow within, but I think the little fellow within the old fellow outside just looks mature and sound mature and affects the world as a mature man; but on the inside, he's just a little boy, innocent, and will never be affected by the praise of the people.

And when death overtakes him, he won't know anything of his so-called greatness. He will only know he is grateful that he was blessed to live to serve a great God, Allah, and a great cause, Islam, and a great teacher, the Honorable Elijah Muhammad.

I was telling Brother Jabril how young people get fame and fortune quickly and lose it almost as quickly as they get it. It destroys them, because it really takes time to produce greatness. Real greatness; just takes time.

And so God, in allowing me to grow, I don't care if millions of people applaud me and cheer me, the little boy inside is oblivious to that. He hardly hears it and that is not his interest. His interest isin the game of marbles; not really marbles but, you know; I just don't know how to explain it."

Historical Timeline of U.S. Government Attacks on The Nation of Islam in America

1939-Security Index of the FBI begins; it will eventually contain 673 members of the Nation of Islam and only 476 members of the Communist party

1942-The Honorable Elijah Muhammad was arrested on charges of sedition

1956-FBI leader J. Edgar Hoover request permission from Attorney General Herbert Brownwell to install surveillance equipment at the home of Elijah Muhammad

1957-Wire taps installed at residence of the Honorable Elijah Muhammad at 4847 S. Woodlawn Avenue in Chicago

1959-The FBI launches a full scale media campaign against the Nation of Islam. This included the use of publications such as Time, U.S. News and World Report, Saturday Evening Post

1961-Wiretap and microphone were installed in the Phoenix residence of the Honorable Elijah Muhammad

1962-FBI begins new counterintelligence initiative by sending anonymous letter to NOI members depicting that the Honorable Elijah Muhammad was living an affluent life while the believers remained poor.

1964-February memo from FBI revealed their plans to foment and exacerbate tensions between Malcolm X and the Honorable Elijah Muhammad.

1965-FBI informants on scene and integral part of the assassination of Malcolm X; memos reveal FBI informants in the top levels of Nation of Islam leadership and within the inner-circle of Malcolm X's OAU and Muslim Mosque Inc. groups

1967-Elijah Muhammad named as target in the newly established COINTELPRO-Black Nationalist Hate Groups program of the FBI. This intensifies and prolongs the FBI's aggressive tactics to neutralize the Nation of Islam. Under COINTELPRO the Nation of Islam was the victim of negative propaganda via bureau friendly journalists; suffered the infiltration of informants and provocateurs; endured its efforts to recruit youthful members being frustrated; and experienced the bureau's use of anonymous mailings to NOI members and leaders that sought to cause members to leave the organization and leaders to fight and hurt one another.

1984-U.S. Senate votes 95-0 to censure Minister Louis Farrakhan

1994-FBI informant Michael Fitzpatrick lures Qubilah Shabazz, daughter of Malcolm X into murder plot against Minister Louis Farrakhan.

2007-Department of Homeland Security admits to illegal surveillance on the Nation of Islam

Minister Farrakhan vs. America's Toughest Minds

(What follows is an analysis of Minister Farrakhan's triumphant victories over the most brilliant minds that American journalism has to offer. It is offered to provide a picture of just who it is that the Minister has faced in public interviews over the years so that we might marvel at how Allah blessed Minister Farrakhan with victory and a growing appeal. None of their training, accomplishments, honors, connections or popularity and confidence could help these journalists succeed in destroying the Minister's magnetism among the people. This is an important fact base in determining how to market Allah's Divine Message that resides within Minister Farrakhan.)

Without Letters but Learned:

The Bible and the Holy Qur'an agree that Jesus is the Messiah. Both books attest to the fact that Jesus was vehemently opposed. From the Biblical narrative, his enemies are categorized as being the Pharisees, Sadducees and the Scribes. According to the Online Etymology Dictionary the word *scribe* is a verb that means *"to write."* In the Hebrew language it is the word *sopher* which means *"writer, scholar."* In Latin its root is from *scribere*, which means "to write." In the Bible's history the Scribes who opposed Jesus were "professional interpreters of the Jewish Law."

So, the history and etymology of the scribes highlights how this group embodied the combination and intersection of the fields of law, writing and the Jewish religion. This connection is relevant and analogous to the profession of journalism in America today. In fact the basic training and education of lawyers and journalists is often identical. This is because undergraduate law students are advised to choose a major that emphasizes research, critical thinking, writing and close reading. In addition, the major media companies in America are headed by Jewish CEOs.

Minister Louis Farrakhan has been handled in the same way that the scribes handled Jesus. In the Bible the Jewish leadership, called *Sanhedrin*, had a meeting that is recorded in St. John Chapter 11. The Bible quotes their fear of Jesus after he had raised Lazarus from death:

"What are we accomplishing?" they asked. "Here is this man performing many miraculous signs. If we let him go on like this, everyone will believe in him, and then the Romans will come and take away both our place and our nation."- St. John 11:47-48(NIV)

The subtitle heading for these verses of scripture is *The Plot to Kill Jesus*. Jesus' crucifixion was therefore planned in the aftermath of his demonstrated ability to give life to the dead. Jesus' crucifixion was planned because the Sanhedrin feared the popularity of Jesus' message. Jesus pointed out their wickedness and their misuse of the people. He condemned their evil monetary practices that had desecrated the holy temples of God. And they saw in Jesus the end of their influence, control and power. So they sought to kill him.

Minister Louis Farrakhan has closely followed Jesus. He has demonstrated the Jesus Leadership Model. And as a result of his desire to follow the Jesus that both Bible and Holy Qur'an call the Messiah, he has acquired unique and extraordinary abilities. This is undeniable. No one enlightens and positively impacts the Black community like the ministry of Minister Louis Farrakhan. In fact, it is not an exaggeration to describe Minister Farrakhan's ministry as indispensable and vitally necessary for Black survival. Minister Farrakhan is to Black America what Islam was to Europe in the Dark Ages. He possesses the guidance, the programmatic thrust and the philosophy necessary to bring the Black community out of our slavery-induced darkness. The historic 1995 Million Man March is one of the many *"miraculous signs"* performed by the Minister that demonstrates this. For in one day the Minister increased voter registration, adoption of Black children; he helped reduce Black on Black crime and sparked an increase in Black men joining community based organizations and houses of worship.

The plot to crucify Minister Farrakhan has always included the effort to destroy his strong appeal and attraction. The strongest and most powerful of journalists have played the part of the modern scribes. They have often been used to try and destroy the magnetism of Minister Farrakhan that, like Jesus, if allowed to continue *"everyone will believe in him."* These mighty journalists who were trained in research, critical thinking, writing and close reading, all were used in a critical aspect of Minister Farrakhan's crucifixion.

Their job was to mock him and make him a caricature. Their job was to poke holes in his message and show his ideas to be unsound and unpopular. But in each case they failed miserably.

None of the celebrated modern scribes were able to accomplish the goal of destroying Minister Farrakhan's magnetism among his people. And what is fascinating and seldom considered is the high levels of formal education held by these celebrity journalists contrasted against the absence of any high level educational degree held by Minister Farrakhan.

Tim Russert of NBC's Meet The Press held a B.A. in Political Science and a Jurist Doctorate also. He was bestowed a total of 48 honorary degrees and was the recipient of the Edward R. Murrow award as well an Emmy award and numerous other awards in journalism.
Mike Wallace of CBS's 60 Minutes also held a B.A. from University of Michigan where an investigative journalism fellowship bears his name. His biography says that he "earned 21 Emmy Awards, five DuPont-Columbia journalism awards, five Peabody awards and the Paul White Award, the most prestigious award given by the Radio and Television News Directors Association. He also won the Robert F. Kennedy Journalism Award grand prize and television first prize in 1996, and was inducted into the Television Academy Hall of Fame in June 1991."
Sam Donaldson graduated from the Mexico Military Institute.
Ted Koppel of ABC's Nightline holds a B.S. degree from Syracuse and an M.A. from Stanford University. A member of the Broadcasting Hall of Fame, Mr. Koppel has won every major broadcasting award including 40 Emmy Awards, eight George Foster Peabody Awards, 10 DuPont-Columbia Awards, and two George Polk Awards. His 10 Overseas Press Club Awards make him the most honored journalist in the Club's history. He has received more than 20 honorary degrees from universities in the United States.
David Broder's bio includes: "He received his bachelor's degree and an M.A. in political science from the University of Chicago. He was a fellow of the Institute of Politics of the John F. Kennedy School of Government

at Harvard University and a fellow of the Institute of Policy Sciences and Public Affairs at Duke University. Broder was awarded the Pulitzer Prize in May 1973 for distinguished commentary. Broder has won numerous awards, including the White Burkett Miller Presidential Award in 1989 and the prestigious 4th Estate Award from the National Press Foundation in 1990, which also honored him with the Distinguished Contributions to Journalism Award in 1993."

Phil Donahue holds a B.A. from University of Notre Dame. He won 9 Emmy Awards and is an inductee into the Academy of Television Arts and Sciences Hall of Fame.

Barbara Walters graduated with an English degree from SaraLawrenceCollege and has won numerous awards.

Cokie Roberts holds a B.A. degree in political science from Wellesley College.

George F. Will- In 1986, the *Wall Street Journal* called him "perhaps the most powerful journalist in America." His biography notes: "Will was educated at Trinity College in Hartford, Connecticut, Oxford University and Princeton University, where he earned his Ph.D. He has taught political philosophy at MichiganStateUniversity, the University of Toronto and Harvard University. In 1977, he won a Pulitzer Prize for commentary for his newspaper columns."

Richard Engel holds a B.A. from Stanford University in international relations. "He speaks and reads fluent Arabic, which he learned while living in Cairo. Engel has also traveled extensively in the Middle East and can comfortably transition between several Arabic dialects spoken across the Arab world. He is also fluent in Italian and Spanish."

Minister Louis Farrakhan went to college but did not complete it. His teacher is the Honorable Elijah Muhammad, whom only completed the third grade. But what Mr. Muhammad taught Minister Farrakhan has equipped him and prepared him in such a way that the sharpest and cleverest of journalists fail in their attempts to derail is powerful message. In fact, amidst his crucifixion at the hands of the modern scribes Minister Farrakhan has routinely enjoyed approval ratings that any politician would envy. Time magazine's cover story in 1994 Ministry of Rage, featured an interview and survey of Minister Farrakhan's appeal and attraction among American Blacks. The surveys found that nearly 2/3 of all Black people agree that Minister Farrakhan speaks the truth!

All that we have written must naturally produce in the minds of Minister Farrakhan's opposers, the same question that the Jews asked about Jesus in the Bible *"How has this man become learned, having never been educated?"*- *John 7:15(NASB)*

Measuring Minister Farrakhan's Electronic Impact

(Top YouTube Clips as of January 31, 2013)

(Every time Minister Farrakhan speaks live and in person, there are thousands of people who come out to see him. Through various YouTube channels, Minister Farrakhan has been able to reach millions of the American people. This extending of Minister Farrakhan's reach has greatly upset his and our enemies. This chart is offered to demonstrate the growing audience of the Minister even though his enemies would like us to believe that his appeal is waning; they want to portray the Nation of Islam as irrelevant. Look at the numbers and see otherwise.)

TITLE	HITS	CHANNEL
Farrakhan warns, advises Obama on Libya	644,701	FCNN
Minister Farrakhan Exposes The Secrets of Freemasonry (1 of 2) (Feb 27, 2011)	546,542	Ahmad770
Minister Louis Farrakhan: State of Black America (Part 1)	444,180	FCNN
Tavis Smiley Questions Minister Farrakhan On President Barack Obama (Part 1 of 5)	414,822	Ahmad770
Snoop Dogg thanks Minister Farrakhan, Nation of Islam for supporting peace, hip hop	378,378	FCNN
Minister Farrakhan Exposes The Secrets of Freemasonry (2 of 2) (Feb 27, 2011)	358,924	Ahmad770
Minister Farrakhan on the Illuminati, The Secret Relationship Between Blacks & Jews, &U.S. History	320,289	Ahmad770
Minister Louis Farrakhan: State of Black America (Part 2)	318,654	FCNN
Farrakhan on "Coalition of Demons" attacking Libya, Africa (June 15, 2011)	280,672	FCNN
Tavis Smiley Questions Minister Louis Farrakhan On President Barack Obama (Part 2 of 5)	238,761	Ahmad770
Farrakhan Exposes Bankers and America's Hidden Agenda	230,934	Ahmad770
Minister Farrakhan's Saviours' Day 2011 Keynote Address	226,072	FCNN
Minister Farrakhan: "That's A Murderer In The White House!"	219,003	Ahmad770
BEST Preaching EVER! Farrakhan Speaks at	215,015	Ahmad770

FellowshipMissionaryBaptistChurch		
Tavis Smiley Questions Minister Louis Farrakhan On President Obama (Part 5 of 5)	212,491	Ahmad770
March 31, 2011 – Farrakhan Press Conference on Libya, Pres. Obama and Col. Gadhafi	209,763	FCNN
Tavis Smiley Questions Minister Louis Farrakhan on President Barack Obama (Part 4 of 5)	201,889	Ahmad770
Tavis Smiley Questions Minister Louis Farrakhan on President Barack Obama (Part 3 of 5)	201,786	Ahmad770
Farrakhan Speaks on Pres. Barack Obama, Judas & the setup of Jesus, Greed, and Zionism	187,099	Ahmad770
Farrakhan responds to Pres. Obama endorsing Gay marriage	186,063	Ahmad770
Farrakhan on LeBron James and Jewish Control (July 11, 2010)	184,954	Ahmad770
Farrakhan responds to charge of anti-Semitism (Al-Jazeera)	174,464	FCNN
Hate rhetoric against Obama & his family – Election 2012	154,450	FCNN
Minister Farrakhan: "Whose Fruit Are We"	153,830	FCNN
Jesus Saves: Exposing The International Bankers	138,892	Ahmad770
Minister Louis Farrakhan Exposes 9/11 and Questions Official Story (Part 1)	136,600	Ahmad770
Minister Farrakhan Blasts Media & Reporters During Interview Commercial!	134,735	Ahmad770
Farrakhan Warns, Advises Obama on Libya	134,231	Ahmad770
Minister Louis Farrakhan Explains The Star of David	132,699	Ahmad770
A Corrupt Government	132,067	Ahmad770
Minister Farrakhan on Ghaddafi & Libya (Feb 27, 2011) (1 of 2)	130,014	Ahmad770
The Untold Story of Hurricane Katrina	124,990	FCNN
Minister Louis Farrakhan asks, "How can you forget?"	124,671	Ahmad770
Minister Farrakhan Lights It Up at Howard University (April 2, 2011)	120,482	Ahmad770
The Fall of The Dollar (The Fall of America)	118,125	Ahmad770
Minister Farrakhan's Prophetic Warning to Wyclef Jean on Leading Haiti	115,806	Ahmad770
The Murder of Malcolm X – What Really Happened?	106,255	FCNN
What Are You Trying To Force Us To Do? PT 1	103,582	Ahmad770
Minister Farrakhan on Ghaddafi & Libya (Feb 27, 2011)(2	102,094	Ahmad770

of 2)		
Impeach Bush Regime for High Crimes (Farrakhan, Al Jazeera)	96,544	FCNN
Louis Farrakhan: The Conspiracy of The International Bankers (Part 1)	96,148	Ahmad770
Louis Farrakhan and Cathy Hughes Interview on TV One (May 9, 2010) – Part 1	94,759	Ahmad770
Farrakhan: Hip Hop & The Power of Cultural Expression	92,764	FCNN
Jewish leaders demand Farrakhan denounce "Secret Relationship" book	86,832	FCNN
Wise Intelligent: Connecting Hip Hop, culture and the struggle	85,993	FCNN
Farrakhan on Obama's signing of NDAA (National Defense Authorization Act)	80,353	FCNN
Farrakhan: President Obama is a "front man: for Criminals	75,773	FCNN
Phil Donahue Interviews Minister Louis Farrakhan	74,469	FCNN
TI Speaks @ Nation of Islam's SD2009	71,508	FCNN
Min. Farrakhan in Chicago Prison (Pt. 1)	71,144	FCNN
Farrakhan Full Speech: War on Libya, Africa (Harlem, NY)	64,463	FCNN
Farrakhan's Exclusive 2013 Interview... Topics: Barack Obama, Django Unchained and more	63,351	FCNN
Farrakhan on Scientology	52,832	FCNN
Farrakhan warns, advises Obama on Libya (1)	44,813	FCNN
The Million Man March Pledge	35,646	FCNN
Farrakhan Exposes the "Black Anti-Semite" Myth	33,717	FCNN
Min. Farrakhan in Chicago Prison (Pt. 2)	32,398	FCNN
Farrakhan addresses American Clergy Leadership Conference	31,666	FCNN
Farrakhan Questioned on Libya & More: WPFW/Pacifica Radio Interview	31,281	FCNN
Minister Farrakhan on Ron Paul & Exposing the Federal Reserve and International Bankers	14,919	Ahmad770

The Best Helper of The Honorable Elijah Muhammad

On the back cover of the book Message To The Blackman in America there is a quote from Reader's Digest that reads as follows: *"This mild-looking man (Elijah Muhammad) is...the most powerful Blackman in America. He offers a new way of life. Muhammad prompts even his severest critics to agree when he says he attacks "traditional reasons the Negro race is weak.""*

There are many acknowledgements of the power, influence and beneficial presence of the Most Honorable Elijah Muhammad like the one above. And all who have marveled at Mr. Muhammad's abilities include their acknowledgement that he was able to accomplish what he did through the many followers that he had throughout America. Getting work done through the efforts of others is the essence of leadership.

The Honorable Elijah Muhammad's most popular helpers and followers were his powerful ministers who allowed Mr. Muhammad to sit in Chicago and direct the activity of temples/mosques, businesses and institutions all over the country. And statistically there was no more prolific, productive and popular minister for Mr. Muhammad than Minister Louis Farrakhan of Muhammad's Temple/Mosque No. 7 in New York City.

Minister Louis Farrakhan served as the Most Honorable Elijah Muhammad's National Representative and Minister of Temple/Mosque No.7 in New York. His work in New York is legendary. In New York City he established 18 temples /mosques of Islam throughout the area of the 5 boroughs. He set up 4 Muhammad Universities of Islam. His average Sunday meeting attendance was 1,000 and his average Wednesday meeting attendance to the mosques was 600 persons coming out to hear him deliver the life-giving teachings of the Most Honorable Elijah Muhammad.

But the most impressive metric of Minister Louis Farrakhan's work in New York is that according to Sepia Magazine, he inspired some 5,000 Black and Hispanic people in New York City to join the Nation of Islam. (Hobbs 1975)

These statistics are critical in quantifying Minister Farrakhan's impact in New York City which was the city that he was assigned to oversee for Mr. Muhammad. But what can't necessarily be quantified is how as the National Representative of the Honorable Elijah Muhammad and the Nation of Islam, he was inspiring thousands to join the Nation of Islam around the country in other cities that aired on local radio stations, Minister Farrakhan's speeches for the Nation of Islam National Radio Broadcast.

Minister Louis Farrakhan is therefore empirically proven to be the best helper that the Honorable Elijah Muhammad had prior to 1975 and post 1975. With respect to New York City, it should be noted that Mr. Muhammad viewed this city as the key city from which he could potentially influence the entire 22 million Black people in America. Consider the following quote from the Most Honorable Elijah Muhammad found in his early series of articles entitled Mr. Muhammad Speaks published inside the pages of the Pittsburgh Courier newspaper.

"Once Harlem is united into the Brotherhood of Islam, she could command the whole 20 million American dark people. She only needs to rid herself of worthless orators who have no constructive program for this half a million dark people. We the Nation of Islam have been given that constructive program and by all means, we intend to give it to our people in Harlem, New York. The readiness in the eyes and actions of the people of Harlem tell you and me that these people are now ready..."

Based on the above quote, it is natural for us to conclude that Mr. Muhammad would assign this key city to his most capable, strongest and productive of ministers. And history proves that this is exactly what he did. The Most Honorable Elijah Muhammad expressed his approval and praise of his minister-Minister Louis Farrakhan- by directing the entire Nation of Islam to continue to 'hear' Minister Farrakhan.

"I want you to pay good attention to his preaching. His preaching is a bearing of witness of me and what God has given to me. This is one of the strongest preachers I have anywhere in the bounds of North America. Everywhere you hear him, listen to him. Everywhere you see him look at him. Everywhere he advises you to go, go. Everywhere he advises you to stay from, stay from. So we are thankful to Allah for this great helper of mine, Minister Farrakhan. He's not a proud man. He's a very humble man. If he can carry you across the lake without dropping you in, he doesn't say when he gets on the other side, "See what I have done?" He tells you, "See what Allah has done." He doesn't take it upon himself. He's a mighty fine preacher. We hear him every week and I say, continue to hear our Minister Farrakhan." -Hon. Elijah Muhammad, July 30 1972, Theology of Time Lecture Series

Today there are those who would feign a love or devotion to the Honorable Elijah Muhammad while condemning his best helper the Honorable Minister Louis Farrakhan. This is a logical fallacy, for how could one love another and hate someone who is the best helper of the one that they love? This defies logic. Especially when you consider that while one could hate Minister Farrakhan; it is Minister Farrakhan who is a better helper of the Honorable Elijah Muhammad; more so than any other person who would even claim to love Mr. Muhammad.

The above quote from the Theology of Time Lecture series used the phrase "continue to hear our Minister Farrakhan." The website Dictionary.com defines the word continue as a verb that means:

"to go on or keep on, as in some course or action; extend; to last or endure; to remain in a particular state or capacity; to remain in a place; abide; stay; to go on with or persist in; to cause to last or endure; maintain or retain, as in a position"

The connotation in the above quote is that followers of the Honorable Elijah Muhammad should continue to listen to, feed from, follow and act in obedience to Minister Louis Farrakhan. Scripturally this is key, considering that the Bible includes a verse of scripture that says "faith comes by hearing and hearing by the word of God."(Romans 10:17). Essentially the Most Honorable Elijah Muhammad is saying that if his followers want to remain faithful, they would find that which would sustain their faith perpetually in the unmatched and unequalled ministry of the Honorable Minister Louis Farrakhan. And I personally bear witness that this is indeed true.

A Timeline of Jewish Attacks Against The Nation of Islam and Minister Farrakhan

- In **1942:** A secret ADL of B'nai Brith file entitled "Temple of Islam Infiltration" states that a "Negro employed by us" prove "quite instrumental" in an FBI raid on the Chicago mosque resulting in 82 arrests.
- In **1959** A Time Magazine article accuses the NOI of "anti-Semitism"
- In response to the **1959** Time Magazine article, the head of the Anti-Defamation League of B'nai B'rith, Arnold Forster, admitted in a secret memo that "Time magazine notwithstanding, we have no documentable evidence of anti-Semitism on the part of the Temples of Islam movement or Elijah Muhammad." He affirmed that they are "not anti-Jewish per se." Yet Jewish organizations publicly continued to label the NOI as anti-Semitic.
- In **1959** The American Jewish Committee sent Black spies from the Urban League to Mr. Muhammad's Newark, New Jersey, appearance.
- In **1960**, the chairman of the American Jewish Congress, Nathan Edelstein, wrote that "We doubt whether the bulk of its followers are presently committed to anti-Semitism." A Jewish scholar Marc Dollinger who studied this racist Jewish phenomenon offered a compelling explanation: "Despite the NOI's political marginalization, American Jewish Committee officials still feared Muhammad. His charismatic personality, willingness to confront racism in the most dramatic rhetorical terms and ability to inspire even non-believing African American listeners concerned Jewish leaders. The NOI leader, they feared, could earn the respect of his Black audiences, even if they chose not to join his movement."
- In **1963:** The Jewish Chronicle of Pittsburgh labeled the NOI "the anti-Semitic Negro extremist group known as the 'Black Muslims.'"
- In **1972** American Jewish Committee under Phillip E. Hoffman release report condemning the "Black Muslims" as using the Muhammad Speaks newspaper to project "a constant drumbeat of inflammatory anti-Zionism and anti-Israel and anti-Semitic propaganda." The report also noted "Only one movement (The

Black Muslims), though looked upon by disfavor by the major black civil rights groups, remains strong, consequential, strong, cohesive, influential and it is a movement that encompasses a significant strain of anti-Semitism.

- In **1984** Nathan Pearlmutter (ADL) referred to Minister Farrakhan as a new *"Black Hitler."* This was in the aftermath of Minister Farrakhan's defense of Rev. Jesse Jackson. The group Jews Against Jackson and its Director Fern Rosenblatt called for the ruining of Rev. Jackson. Rev. Jackson also suffered firebombing of his campaign offices.
- In **1984**, when The Honorable Minister Louis Farrakhan was censured by the United States Senate in a 95-0 vote for alleged acts of anti-Semitism. The charge of anti-Semitism served to thwart the Nation of Islam Security companies; the POWER Products personal care line; and the National African American Leadership Conference (NAALS)

Minister Farrakhan as a Defender of Black People

(Throughout the years Minister Farrakhan's love for Black People has been witnessed as he has looked beyond their faults and ministered unto their needs. Below is a listing of many of those who have been beneficiaries of Minister Farrakhan's defense. These episodes in the history show Minister Farrakhan using his good name and reputation to defend prominent Blacks who have found themselves in trouble. Jewish author Daniel Pipes commented on this phenomenon in a blog post on his website; an excerpt from his blog post is below)

"The *New York Post* reports today that "Michael Jackson last night became a member of the Nation of Islam." Of course, this development takes place in the aftermath of Jackson's being arrested on Nov. 20 in connection with child-molestation charges and now being out on $3 million bail.

If this report of his conversion proves to be accurate, it would fit a well-established pattern of African-Americans who, finding their reputation in tatters, turn to the Nation of Islam, which then provides them with solace and help. This phenomenon is most apparent in jails, where blacks since the late 1940s have been converting in large numbers. Famous converts in trouble include:

- *Tawana Brawley*, who converted after her much-publicized claim of being raped by a gang of white men turned out to be a hoax;
- *Mike Tyson*, the heavyweight champion jailed for rape,
- *Benjamin Chavis*, who converted after his eviction from the National Association for the Advancement of Colored People, in large part for having paid off a mistress with NAACP funds.
- *Kenny Gamble*, the music producer whose life fell apart as he faced a payola investigation in 1975.

Other blacks in disgrace do not make the full step to conversion but become closely affiliated with the NOI, which provides them too with political and moral support. Prominent beneficiaries include:

- *Alcee Hastings*, an impeached Federal judge;

- *Marion Barry*, the mayor of Washington, D.C., convicted for drug-taking;
- *George Stallings*, a Catholic priest accused of child molestation; and
- *Gus Savage*, a U.S. congressman from Illinois charged with sexual harassment.

Finally, some blacks in difficult straits merely dip into Islam, without developing a formal relationship – such as O.J. Simpson, who read the Qur'an while incarcerated."

-Daniel Pipes; December 18, 2003, updated Jun 27, 2010
http://www.danielpipes.org/blog/2003/12/michael-jackson-and-blacks-in-stress-who

1. Mayor Marion Barry
2. Mike Tyson
3. Rev. Jesse Jackson
4. Michael Jackson
5. O.J. Simpson
6. Rep. Alcee Hastings
7. Julian Bond
8. Rep. Cynthia McKinney
9. Rep. Earl Hilliard
10. Tawana Brawley
11. David Dinkins
12. President Barak Obama
13. Rev. Charles Coen
14. Rev. Eddie Carthan
15. Qubilah Shabazz
16. Malcolm Shabazz
17. Charles Rangel
18. Congressman Mel Reynolds
19. Mayor Willie Herenton
20. Congressional Black Caucus
21. Mayor Kwame Kilpatrick
22. Benjamin Chavis
23. James Luther Bevel
24. Father Michael Pfleger
25. Rev. T.L. Barrett
26. Alderman Dorothy Tillman
27. Harold Washington Cultural Center
28. Imam Jamil Al-Amin (H.Rap Brown)
29. Bloods and Crips
30. Vice Lords and Gangster Disciples
31. From Gangs to Street Organizations
32. Hip-Hop Community
33. Stan Tookie Williams
34. Sistah Souljah
35. Bishop George A. Stallings
36. Rep. Bobby Rush
37. Steve Cokely
38. Arsenio Hall
39. Bill Cosby
40. Oprah Winfrey
41. Harold-Washington

Stoned for Good Works, Propaganda Keeps Hidden Minister Farrakhan's Stellar Record of Leadership

Jesus answered them, Many good works have I showed you from my Father; for which of those works do ye stone me? —John 10:32 KJV

It is ugly and egregious that Minister Louis Farrakhan's current campaign to promote peace in the streets is being attached to an alleged history of anti-Semitism. Nearly every publication that has covered the Minister's efforts has felt the need to rehash baseless lies, seeking to destroy the magnetism between the Minister and the People.

When watching the love, excitement and admiration of Black people who live in the crime-ridden streets of Chicago to the live, physical presence of Minister Farrakhan, one can't help but think of another legendary Black man who made his ministry in the "highways and byways"—Jesus of Nazareth. The New Testament records that it was the poor who "heard him (Jesus) gladly. (Mark 12:37)"

Back then it was the Jewish Sanhedrin that opposed Jesus' public ministry. Today it is the ADL and its Zionist affiliates that oppose Minister Farrakhan. The Bible's history of Jesus is very important in any analysis of the phenomenal presence of Minister Louis Farrakhan. This is because Minister Farrakhan is unique. Most religious and secular leaders within America's Judeo-Christian landscape are comfortable deifying Jesus as an object of worship. Minister Farrakhan as a Muslim enacts what can be defined as a Jesus Leadership Model. The Jesus Leadership Model is characterized by a leader's ability to demonstrate self-sacrifice, longsuffering, courage and magnetism.

Much of what Minister Farrakhan and the Nation of Islam have suffered at the hands of the Jewish/Zionist leadership is detailed in the preface of the book *The Secret Relationship Between Blacks and Jews, Volume 2 (TSRV2)*. *The Secret Relationship between Blacks and Jews* contains eye-opening revelations and records of the Anti-Defamation League of B'nai B'rith admitting in internal memos that the NOI is not anti-Semitic, while at the same time publicly leading a smear campaign against the "Black Muslims," falsely labeling the NOI "anti-Semitic."

"*Time* magazine notwithstanding, we have no documentable evidence of anti-Semitism on the part of the Temples of Islam movement or Elijah Muhammad." —*Arnold Forster, ADL President*

"We doubt whether the bulk of its (NOI) followers are presently committed to anti-Semitism." —*Nathan Edelstein, American Jewish Congress chairman*

The above quotes are Jewish admissions that their hatred of the NOI did not arise out of any legitimate cause for concern.

Jewish scholar Marc Dollinger is quoted in the book. He offers an explanation as to why these Jewish groups were "hating" on the Honorable Elijah Muhammad. Dollinger writes: *"Despite the Nation of Islam's political marginalization, American Jewish Committee officials still feared Muhammad. His charismatic personality, willingness to confront racism in the most dramatic rhetorical terms and ability to inspire even non-believing African American listeners concerned Jewish leaders. The Nation of Islam leader, they feared, could earn the respect of his black audiences, even if they chose not to join his movement."*

The more recent history of Minister Louis Farrakhan details how he has been feared and attacked in the same way as his teacher the Honorable Elijah Muhammad. Remember that in 1984 the Reverend Jesse Jackson campaigned for the presidency of the United States of America. At that time *Time* magazine reported: *"A group called Jews Against Jackson...pledged publicly to disrupt his candidacy. Two of its members were arrested for interrupting his announcement speech on Nov. 3 in Washington, D.C. A window in Jackson's New Hampshire campaign headquarters in Manchester was smashed, and his campaign offices in Garden Grove, Calif., were fire bombed. Jackson's life has been threatened."* To this Minister Farrakhan responded to defend Reverend Jackson: *"If you harm this brother, I warn you in the name of Allah this will be the last one you harm. Leave this servant of God alone."*

Following his courageous defense of Reverend Jackson, Minister Farrakhan began being attacked by a multiplicity of Jewish voices. Nathan Pearlmutter of the Anti-Defamation League of B'nai B'rith (ADL) and Nat Hentoff of the *Village Voice* referred to Minister Farrakhan as a new *"Black Hitler."*

This began Minister Farrakhan's crucifixion on the cross. In Roman times, crucifixion on the cross was meant for pain and humiliation. And while the charge of anti-Semitism is meant to embarrass and injure the public profile of the person so charged, it also signifies the crossing out, thwarting, undermining and sabotaging of Minister Farrakhan's plans to help suffering Black America. In other words, the Zionists set out to murder the Minister's plans and programs.

Minister Farrakhan was pinned with a crown of thorns when in 1984, pressure from Jewish groups caused the United States Senate to vote 95-0 to censure Minister Farrakhan for alleged acts of anti-Semitism. The crown of thorns put on the head of Jesus signified that instead of being adorned with the honor, dignity and respect of a royal crown, Jesus would be mocked and ridiculed and suffer the pain of the thorns of a false crown. The modern Sanhedrin sought to falsely crown Minister Farrakhan with an official, governmental designation—"anti-Semite."

Jesus, according to the Bible, had his hands nailed down and Minister Farrakhan had his economic initiatives destroyed. Jesus was a carpenter by trade, so to nail down his hands was to hinder his ability to construct, build and repair. This would destroy a man who made his living through the work of his hands. And even though Jesus gave up his profession to devote himself to his ministry, it is easy to see that the nailing of his hands would destroy him economically. Symbolically, the Jewish leadership has thwarted the Minister's ability to build up the Black community spiritually and economically.

And every time Minister Farrakhan begins an economic program, his efforts are stymied by the ADL and those that it controls. When Minister Farrakhan received a $5 million dollar loan from an African head of state, Libyan leader Muammar Gadhafi, he started a personal care product line called P.O.W.E.R. (People Organized Working for Economic Rebirth). His purpose for the funds was to develop an economic base in the very lucrative Black hair and personal care product industry. This initiative was crossed out when Jewish distributors threatened Mr. George Johnson of Johnson Products that they would not distribute his products any longer if he followed through on his agreement to Minister Farrakhan to manufacture the products. In addition, because of Jewish pressure the Black-owned Independence Bank of Chicago demanded that the Minister take the $5 million dollars that he deposited with them out of their bank.

As part of his crucifixion Jesus was pierced in the side of his body. In Minister Farrakhan's case it was the body of his organization. His followers and the communities they serve suffered when the ADL pressured the U.S. Housing and Urban Development (HUD) to end security contracts with NOI Security. Many remember when the male members of the Nation of Islam organized themselves to perform security patrols in some of the most drug-infested and crime-ridden apartment complexes in the country. The Muslim brothers of the Fruit of Islam (FOI) established security companies to provide safety and security to poor people living in public housing. But Jewish pressure on the Congress thwarted this successful economic and social services initiative by the Nation of Islam. Republican Jack Kemp and former first lady Barbara Bush were among many who praised the Nation of Islam for their work in securing vulnerable neighborhoods.

This analogy concludes by considering the interference Jewish groups have made to hinder Minister Farrakhan's movement among his people. This can be likened to nailing his feet to the cross. And when one's feet are nailed, movement is hindered. Minister Farrakhan's desire has been to go among his people to teach them and to bring them a better quality of life. His desire has been to make the Black man and woman of America the equal of the best of civilized people. There are many examples of Jewish groups protesting the leaders Black people choose to listen to and follow. A classic example of this is when in 1993 Minister Farrakhan was disinvited to speak at the 30th anniversary of the March on Washington. He was invited initially and then disinvited after Rabbi David Saperstein complained. The Black organizers of that march gave in. They disinvited the man whom divine providence blessed two years later to convene the largest March in American history—the Million Man March.

The case of Minister Louis Farrakhan's crucifixion is part of the terrible legacy of the Crucifixion of Black Leadership. It's time for our affliction to end.

The Crucifixion of Black Jesus

History's "Dark-Skinned" Revolutionaries, Their Shared Values, Shared Enemies and Shared Fate

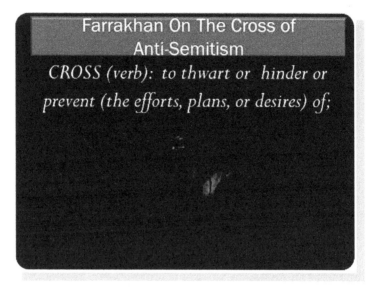

I can remember as a child growing up and at an early age becoming acquainted with the mentality of Black self-hatred that has become a cultural norm among Black people in America. The hatred of Black skin, kinky black hair and in general all physical features deemed African among the very people who possess those features is unfortunately not unusual in Black communities even in 2010. As I write this I refer to incidences when children called other children things like "Black Jesus" or "Black African." You could often hear this whenever any kind of juvenile name calling was done for amusement or meanness.

Now for young children in the 80's "checking" one another with insults like "Black Jesus" indicated a fundamental and formerly long held belief that the real Jesus was White.

Jesus is an important figure in Christianity, Judaism and Islam. In the Black community he is of extreme importance because most Blacks in this country self-identify as being Christian. There are numerous Churches and denominations of Christianity that make up the religious landscape of America's inner-cities and suburbs. In fact on the mantle piece of many elderly Black people's homes is a picture of John F. Kennedy, Dr. Martin L. King Jr., and "Jesus". The myriad of pastors, ministers, reverends and bishops stand in their pulpits and, among other matters, articulate the plan of salvation that involves a belief in Jesus as the Son of God and that he was crucified for the sins of the world, and that he was raised from the dead and ascended into heaven to be with God the Father.

There is however a problem with what is taught and understood concerning Jesus. The leading religious scholars and theologians find it difficult to reconcile the history of Jesus with what is written in the New Testament of the Bible. In a book titled The 5 Gospels the leading researchers and professors in the field of study devoted to the life of Jesus write that 82% of what is attributed as being the words of Jesus in the New Testament, the historical Jesus never said! This group including Dr. Robert Funk, Karen Armstrong, John Dominic Crossan and about 150 other scholars call themselves the Jesus Seminar. They attribute that 84% of the deeds attributable to Jesus in the New Testament were never done by the actual man Jesus of 2000 years ago!

The conclusions of the Jesus Seminar are consistent with what Dr. Patricia Eddy writes in her book Who Tampered With the Bible? *"What is not generally understood, however, is that individual evangelists and sects actually altered the words and actions of Jesus to fit their own purposes."* Both of these books are witness bearers to the Honorable Elijah Muhammad and Honorable Minister Louis Farrakhan who say in the point No. 3 of What The Muslims Believe that "the Bible has been tampered with and must be reinterpreted so that mankind will not be snared by the falsehoods added to it.

Ethnicity of Jesus
If Jesus was white then none of us in the Black community would be upset. After all, we have lived thinking that he was white at least since the days of Black slavery in America. However Dr. Robert Eisler cites Jewish Historian Flavius Josephus' physical description of Jesus:
"Both his nature and his form were human: for he was a man of simple appearance, mature age, short growth, three cubits tall [about 4 and a half feet, based on the Jewish cubit], with scanty hair, but having a line in the

*middle of the head after the fashion of the Naziraeans, eyebrows meeting above the nose so that the spectators could take fright, with a long face, a long nose, and with an undeveloped beard, **dark skin**, and hunchbacked." (The Messiah Jesus and John the Baptist According to Flavius Josephus, Robert Eisler, Ph.D.; The Dial Press, New York; pp. 425-429)*

This is a historical physical description of Jesus as a short "dark skin" man. But despite the tampering throughout the Bible, this description is consistent with the various clues in the Bible of Jesus physical description. John, on the isle of Patmos in the book of Revelations describes Jesus as having feet the color of burnish brass and hair like wool (Rev1:14-15). The Gospels describe him as being of the seed of David (Romans 1:3) according to the flesh and declared to be the son of God. If this is so then Solomon who is David's son and therefore an ancestor of Jesus is described as being "black but comely (handsome) o you daughters of Jerusalem (Song of Solomon 1:5)." Another clue of Jesus ethnicity is that while the census was being taken and Herod had decreed to kill all boy babies Mary and Joseph were able to hide in Egypt(Matthew 2:13)

Judge A Man By The Quality Of His Enemies
There is an old saying that you don't judge a man by who his friends are but you judge a man by the quality of his enemies. In the Holy Quran Allah says in Surah 6 Verse (Ayat) *112: "And thus did We make for every prophet an enemy, the devils from among men and jinn, some of them inspiring others with gilded speech to deceive (them). And if thy Lord pleased, they would not do it, so leave them alone with what they forge"*

Jesus in the New Testament has a public ministry of 3 and ½ years. During that short time period he had angered several significant sectors of power and drawn out the enemies that, at least from the Qur'anic perspective, were made by Allah (God) for his own special purposes. If they were made by Allah, God, then they are not ordinary enemies. It is easy to understand that an enemy made by Allah, the supreme being, who is all-wise(al-Hakim) and is referred to in the Holy Quran as the Best Knower would be an enemy whose strength and power would be in proportion to the strength and power that Allah, the supreme being, would deposit within the prophet. Therefore, Jesus in the scripture can be deemed a tremendously powerful and influential figure because his enemies and opposers were the most powerful entities of his day. Within the ranks of the Jewish community were arrayed the Pharisees, Sadducees and Scribes. The New Testament states that Jesus was tried at the home of the High Priest Caiaphas and found guilty. And in the final drama we see the alliance between the Roman authorities and the Jewish Sanhedrin Council to crucify Jesus- the righteous teacher.

Why was Jesus so vehemently opposed? Or better yet why am I writing about it in 2010? There are literally scores of volumes of scholastic literature on this subject from a variety of prolific scholars and writers from around the globe. From my vantage point, there is however no connection made in the available literature between Jesus' crucifixion and the crucifixion of Blacks in America, particularly the "dark-skinned" revolutionary men who comprise Jesus' modern ethnic bretheren.

The Honorable Minister Louis Farrakhan is such a "dark-skin" revolutionary. We might not consider him "dark-skin" in a literal way as much as we can definitely acknowledge him as being a revolutionary voice and personage raised from among the literally "dark-skinned" people. He is opposed like Jesus by certain Jewish leaders and is opposed by certain governmental divisions as well.

I should note at this time that the New Testament does not reveal any legitimate reason for the opposition to Jesus. In fact in the 3rd Chapter of John we read that the Sanhedrin Council knew Jesus had been sent by God! "*1Now there was a man of the Pharisees named Nicodemus, a member of the Jewish ruling council. 2He came to Jesus at night and said, "Rabbi, we know you are a teacher who has come from God. For no one could perform the miraculous signs you are doing if God were not with him."(NIV)*

Lazarus As The Mentally Dead Black Masses

In the 11th Chapter of John we are further exposed to the illegitimate nature of the plot to kill Jesus. It was after Jesus had raised Lazarus from the dead that we read of the Sanhedrin Council's sinister plot. *47Then the chief priests and the Pharisees called a meeting of the Sanhedrin. "What are we accomplishing?" they asked. "Here is this man performing many miraculous signs. 48If we let him go on like this, everyone will believe in him, and then the Romans will come and take away both our place and our nation." (John 11:47-48 NIV).*

It is significant that it was after the resurrection of Lazarus when the plot to kill Jesus was put into action. Lazarus was believed to be dead, but Jesus said that he wasn't dead, he was just only sleeping. Jesus then begins to raise him through the word of his mouth, which suggests that Jesus was correct in his initial assessment.

Black people in America were once called Negroes. The word Negro in Latin is the same as the word "Necro" which means 'death'. "Necro" is a common prefix for words relational in some way to death (i.e. Necrosis, necropolis, necrophilia). It might be understandable that Blacks would be dubbed Negroes (Dead) in light of the process employed to make of proud, independent Africans the chattel slaves of America. Most who have only a cursory knowledge of slavery are familiar with the slave traders and the slave masters but don't know much of the most crucial functionary in the Transatlantic Slave Trade, "the slave maker." It was his sinister work of taking the African and breaking him mentally the same way wild animals are broken. This process of breaking the African mentally was celebrated and touted as an accomplishment by Senator Henry Berry on the floor of the Virginia House of Delegates when he stated in 1832: *"we have as far as possible closed every avenue by which light may enter the slaves mind. If we could extinguish the capacity to see the light our work would be complete. They would then be on the level of the beast of the field and we would be safe."* The mental death produced by the "closing of every avenue of light" or learning that took place during slavery is therefore comparable to the "sleeping" death that Lazarus experienced in the New Testament. Jesus then was able to awaken him from his death (sleep) with the right combination and configuration of words likewise the resurrection from mental death of Blacks in America would be by means of the right combination and configuration of words.

The Honorable Elijah Muhammad has been quoted as saying "what I have given you is a wake-up message." The master of that wake-up message and as a result the principal raiser of the mentally dead Black masses is the Honorable Minister Louis Farrakhan. This is an undisputable claim especially when you consider the 1995 Million Man March which produced approximately 1.8 million men on the mall in Washington, D.C. This, the largest gathering on the mall in American history, signaled an awakening of

Black men to the values atonement, reconciliation and responsibility which are the very antithesis of the values deemed necessary for them to be made slaves and members of the permanent underclass. To be a slave and a member of the permanent underclass requires self-destructive, irreverent and irresponsible attributes that are often apparent in many sectors of the Black community today.

COINTELPRO As The Modern Roman Authorities

In reality it was J. Edgar Hoover, the infamous 20th Century leader of the F.B.I. who headed up the infamous counterintelligence program (COINTELPRO) that used the language "messiah" in his memorandums that outlaid what became known as denial objectives aimed at neutralizing all major Black leaders and organizations. To achieve these ends he utilized the tremendous financial resources of the U.S. Government to disrupt, frustrate and extinguish the efforts made by "dark-skin" revolutionaries and the various Black organizations they led. Marcus Garvey, Dr. Martin Luther King Jr., Stokely Carmichael, Malcolm X, Honorable Elijah Muhammad, Huey Newton, Maulana Karenga and others of their kind were all targets of the U.S. Government. From Hoover's vantage point the position of Black leader was the de facto position of Messiah and that meant each Black leader and organization was marked for crucifixion. As for Minister Farrakhan and the Nation of Islam, the Department of Homeland Security as recent as 2007 appeared to be operating from the deceased Hoover's playbook when it was found to be illegally targeting the NOI for domestic espionage.

The FBI under Hoover utilized what can be considered a modern, sophisticated form of crucifixion. We should remember that crucifixion, as it is detailed in the New Testament, was a public form of punishment, designed to not only inflict pain and death upon its victims but also humiliation. This kind of harsh execution, death on the cross, not only killed the victim but also killed their reputation and created for them a perpetual "dishonorable mention" in the minds of the spectating public. Crucifixion on the cross was to put fear in the hearts of the people and demonstrate what would become of any who dared to believe in and follow the revolutionary leader. It can be argued that the public humiliation, disgrace and fear it produced was the real object of the crucifixion since the fear of the revolutionary leaders was never based on any history of violence or crime. The real fear is that the popularity of the revolutionary leader grows to the point where the "whole world will believe in him" and adopt his cause as their cause, his mind as their mind and thereby rendering the applecart of oppression irreparably upset.

Consider the following excerpted from FBI internal memorandum that spelled out the COINTELPRO activities aimed at Black Nationalist organizations:

"The purpose of this new counterintelligence endeavor is to expose, disrupt, misdirect, discredit, or otherwise neutralize the activities of Black Nationalist, hate-type organizations and groupings, their leadership, spokesmen, membership, and supporters, and to counter their propensity for violence and civil disorder.

The pernicious background of such groups, their duplicity, and devious maneuvers must be exposed to public scrutiny where such publicity will have a neutralizing effect. Efforts of the various groups to consolidate their forces or to recruit new or youthful adherents must be frustrated. No opportunity should be missed to exploit through counterintelligence techniques the organizational and personal conflicts of the leaderships of the groups and where possible an effort should be made to capitalize upon existing conflicts between competing Black Nationalist organizations. When an opportunity is apparent to disrupt or neutralize black nationalist, hate-type organizations through the cooperation of established local news media contacts or through such contact with sources available to the Seat of Government, in every instance careful attention must be given to the proposal to insure the targeted group is disrupted, ridiculed, or discredited through the publicity and not merely publicized.

Intensified attention under this program should be afforded to the activities of such groups as the Student Nonviolent Coordinating Committee, the Southern Christian Leadership Conference, Revolutionary Action Movement, the Deacons for Defense and Justice, Congress of Racial Equality, and the Nation of Islam. Particular emphasis should be given to extremists who direct the activities and policies of revolutionary or militant groups such as Stokely Carmichael, H. "Rap" Brown, Elijah Muhammad, and Maxwell Stanford." (From Director to 23 Field Offices, Aug. 26, 1967)

In another memorandum courtesy of the Freedom of Information Act we see the ramping up of the COINTELPRO activities with the specifics of the desired outcomes detailed:

"The Counterintelligence Program is now being expanded to include 41 offices. ... For maximum effectiveness of the Counterintelligence Program, and to prevent wasted effort, long range goals are being set.

1. Prevent the coalition of militant Black Nationalist groups. In unity there is strength; a truism that is no less valid for all its triteness. An effective coalition of Black Nationalist groups might be the first step toward a real "Mau Mau" in America, the beginning of a true black revolution.

2. Prevent the rise of a "messiah" who could unify, and electrify, the militant Black Nationalist movement. Malcolm X might have been such a "messiah;" he is the martyr of the movement today. Martin Luther King, Stokely Carmichael and Elijah Muhammad all aspire to this position. Elijah Muhammad is less of a threat because of his age. King could be a very real contender for this position should he abandon his supposed "obedience" to "white, liberal doctrines" (nonviolence) and embrace Black Nationalism. Carmichael has the necessary charisma to be a real threat in this way.

3. Prevent violence on the part of Black Nationalist groups. This is of primary importance, and is, of course, a goal of our investigative activity; it should also be a goal of the Counterintelligence Program. Through counterintelligence it should be possible to pinpoint potential troublemakers and neutralize them before they exercise their potential for violence.

4. Prevent militant Black Nationalist groups and leaders from gaining respectability, by discrediting them to three separate segments of the community. The goal of discrediting black nationalists must be handled tactically in three ways. You must discredit these groups and individuals to, first, the responsible Negro community. Second, they must be discredited to the white community, both the responsible community and to "liberals" who have vestiges of sympathy for militant black nationalists simply because they are Negroes. Third, these groups must be discredited in the eyes of Negro radicals, the followers of the movement. This last area requires entirely different tactics from the first two. Publicity about violent tendencies and radical statements merely enhances black nationalists to the last group; it adds "respectability" in a different way.

5. A final goal should be to prevent the long-range growth of militant Black Nationalist organizations, especially among youth. Specific tactics to prevent these groups from converting young people must be developed." (From Director to Field Offices on March 4, 1968)

This modern, sophisticated form of crucifixion created for the "dark-skin" revolutionaries of the Black liberation struggle the same fate as their ethnic big brother Jesus. For Malcolm X and Dr. Martin Luther King Jr. it was assassination and the subsequent corruption of their message and mission. For Marcus Garvey it was deportation. Paul Robeson and W.E.B. Dubois suffered character assassination and economic ruin. Strong Black Organizations like the Black Panther Party, SNCC, Us, Republic of New Africa and the Nation of Islam all suffered government funded infiltration and thwarting.

Jewish Leadership As The Modern Sanhedrin Council
In the same way that Jesus death on the cross was the fruit of the collaboration between the Roman authorities and the Sanhedrin Jewish leadership, the modern Jesuses of today were put on the path to crucifixion via the collaboration of the U.S. Government and the modern Sanhedrin Council. Most in the Black community would be surprised to learn that the Honorable Minister Louis Farrakhan is not the only leader tagged as being anti-Semitic. The Secret Relationship Between Blacks and Jews Volume 2 records the history of many of our great heroes and heroines branded with the much feared designation of "anti-Semite." Page x of TSRV2 lists Booker T. Washington, W.E.B. Dubois, Marcus Garvey, Dr. Martin Luther King Jr., Malcolm X, Honorable Elijah Muhammad, President Nelson Mandela, Bishop Desmond Tutu, Julian Bond, Kwame Ture, Andrew Young, Kweisi Mfume, and Rev. Al. Sharpton and Rev. Jesse Jackson and Rev. Joseph Lowery. "Learned Black scholars like John Hope Franklin, J.A. Rogers, James Baldwin, Richard Wright, Julius Lester and Alice Walker have all been castigated as "black anti-Semites." Black entertainers like Michael Jackson, Spike Lee, Ice Cube, Arsenio Hall, Muhammad Ali, Public Enemy, and even

Oprah Winfrey, if we are to believe some Jewish spokespeople, are all "black anti-Semites."

Why is being labeled an anti-Semite so feared a fate? It is because that is the means of the discrediting and ridiculing called for in the COINTELPRO memos. The accusation of anti-Semitism is used as a sophisticated form of 'crucifixion on the cross.' Consider the dictionary meaning of the word cross as a verb that means to *thwart: hinder or prevent (the efforts, plans, or desires) of.* It is no secret that having that designation attached to one's reputation thwarts their personal progress and can prevent the fruition of their plans and desires. The reason for this can be traced to Biblical scripture when one acknowledges its influential role in shaping the thinking of people in a Judeo-Christian society. The Bible in several passages says that if you bless the children of Israel, God will bless you; and if you curse the children of Israel, God will curse you. *"I will bless those who bless you, and whoever curses you I will curse; and all peoples on earth will be blessed through you." Genesis 12:3 (see also Genesis12:29, Numbers 24:9 and 22:6, Exodus 23:22).*

The Honorable Minister Louis Farrakhan has done a series of 3 speeches that essentially grow out of What the Muslims Believe Point number 5 which states "*...Furthermore, we believe we are the people of God's choice, as it has been written, that God would choose the rejected and the despised. We can find no other persons fitting this description in these last days more than the so-called Negroes in America.*" The series of speeches entitled The Real Children of Israel (parts 1-3) brings history, scripture and empirical data to showcase and defend the Honorable Elijah Muhammad's original thesis articulated in point number 5 that the Black people of America are the actual fulfillment of those afore mentioned Biblical prophecies.

We have shown in this series of articles that historically speaking the Jesus who was born among the children of Israel in scripture was a "dark-skin" revolutionary. Dr. Obery Hendricks, Professor of Biblical Interpretation at New York Theological Seminary and author of the new book *The Politics of Jesus: Rediscovering the True Revolutionary Nature of Jesus' Teachings and How They Have Been Corrupted* describes the revolutionary nature of Jesus teaching. Among the 7 components of Jesus revolutionary message uncovered by Dr. Hendricks in his excellent book are "treat the people's needs as holy," "give a voice to the voiceless" and "expose the workings of oppression" or to challenge the established order of things. The Black Jesuses that are the historical Jesus' modern ethnic brethren and who are mentioned in this article are further united with him in a brotherhood of shared values and revolutionary principles governing the work they have labored to do among Black people in America. These are the principles that I find particularly shared between Jesus and the Honorable Minister Louis Farrakhan.

In the final analysis the Black community cannot afford to just be praisers of Jesus without learning the important lessons in the history of Jesus and its parallels to Black history in America. But how can our community learn these lessons if our community does not at the same time give birth to those who are willing to teach and share wisdom with their people? How many of us will determine that within our own circles of familiarity and influence that we will become a Jesus and become revolutionary to the ignorance and self-destruction that has become the status quo of Black life in America today. I pray that if you found value in this series of articles that you will share it with someone you love.

From Fard to Farrakhan: America's Punishment of Messianic Dissidents

Allah loves not the public utterance of hurtful speech, except by one who has been wronged. And Allah is ever Hearing, Knowing.

--Holy Qur'an 4: 148 (M.M. Ali Translation)

Can wicked rulers be allied with you, those who frame injustice by statute?

--Psalms 94:20(ESV)

"I confidently trust that the American people will prove themselves ... too wise not to detect the false pride or the dangerous ambitions or the selfish schemes which so often hide themselves under that deceptive cry of mock patriotism: 'Our country, right or wrong!' They will not fail to recognize that our dignity, our free institutions and the peace and welfare of this and coming generations of Americans will be secure only as we cling to the watchword of *true* patriotism: 'Our country—when right to be kept right; when wrong to be put right.'"

—Schurz, "The Policy of Imperialism," *Speeches, Correspondence and Political Papers of Carl Schurz,* vol. 6, pp. 119–20 (1913).

Congress shall make no law respecting an establishment of religion, or prohibiting the free exercise thereof; or abridging the freedom of speech, or of the press; or the right of the people peaceably to assemble, and to petition the Government for a redress of grievances.

—First Amendment, U.S. Constitution

Narrated by Abu Sa'id al-Khudri: The Prophet (pbuh) said: The best fighting (jihad) in the path of Allah is (to speak) a word of justice to an oppressive ruler.

—Hadith of Prophet Muhammad (pbuh) Abu Dawud Collection Book 32, Hadith Number 4330.

The Honorable Elijah Muhammad taught that his teacher, Master Fard Muhammad began coming in and out of America in the year 1910. He was studying the American social, political, religious and economic landscape. Among the many things he did included him living with a Caucasian family for a while as well as studying at the University of Southern California. He would travel in and out of America for 20 years before the most important aspect of His work would commence in "Black Bottom" Detroit, Michigan. In Detroit he began to teach Black people Islam with what many have described as a strange methodology. In September 1931 he met Elijah Poole, who became the Honorable Elijah Muhammad, and began to teach him night and day for 3 years and 4 months. This master-student relationship would prove to be of extreme importance as it was the beginnings of the most influential religious group anywhere in America, the Nation of Islam.

There has not been a lot of attention on the NOI's positive influence in the areas of free speech and dissent. But the Nation of Islam founder, in addition to establishing a religious tradition simultaneously produced a very significant protest movement. Within the Nation of Islam it is believed that Master Fard Muhammad is the source of what Lothrop Stoddard called "the rising tide of color" which moved throughout Africa and the world to stimulate and inspire the darker races to revolt against the evils of European Colonialism.

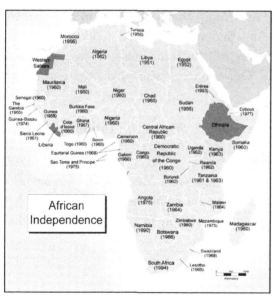

Muslims believe this because of what has been taught about the world travels of Master Fard Muhammad, *"He told me that he had traveled the world over and that he had visited North America for 20 years before making himself known to us, his people whom he came for. He had visited the Isles of the Pacific, Japan and China, Canada, Alaska, The North Pole, India, Pakistan, All of the Near East and Africa...He visited every inhabited place on the*

earth..." (Hon. Elijah Muhammad, Pittsburgh Courier 7, 20, 1957). The aftermath of Fard's travels is an amazing season in the 20th Century where former European colonies, in Africa and elsewhere, fought to gain their freedom. Even the historic Bandung Conference of 1955, 400 years from the beginning of the Black American sojourn in slavery, bears the imprint of Fard's thinking. The Bandung Conference reflected a dominant theme of Nation of Islam teaching that articulates that the time has arrived in world history for the Black nation, including all the darker races of man, to rise up, unite, and throw off the yoke of European tyranny and oppression; this was a global conference where no white European countries were permitted.

There is much to be written and taught about the global impact of the mysterious man from Mecca-Master Wali Fard Muhammad. Within the Nation of Islam the revolutionary aftermath of his world travels fits within the eschatological description of the Bible's Habakkuk chapter 3. Habakkuk 3 paints a picture of a revolutionary theophany, where the God of the enslaved Children of Israel visits them and punishes their enemies with plagues, and disaster.

Inside of America Master Fard Muhammad's mission influenced many from all races to become criers, warners and protestors of America's unjust foreign wars and corrosive domestic racism. His agitation of the poor masses angered local and federal authorities, and many who were inspired by Master Fard Muhammad's teaching were arrested and imprisoned for simply exercising the constitutionally guaranteed right to dissent or disagree with the U.S. government. Author Ernest Allen Jr. documents the history of messianic dissent among Blacks in America in his report entitled *When Japan Was Champion of The Darker Races: Satokata Takahashi and The Flowering of Black Messianic Nationalism.* An excerpt from Allen's report includes: "*In late September 1942, in a series of highly publicized raids, federal agents in Chicago arrested eighty-five African Americans. Three women and nine men were charged with sedition; the remainder were accused of draft evasion. Indicted on the former charge(sedition) were Elijah Muhammad, Linn Karriem, and Pauline Bahar of the Allah Temple of Islam [ATOI]; Mittie Maud Lena Gordon, Sean Jones, William Gordon, and David J. Logan of the Peace Movement of Ethiopia [PME]; Charles Newby (aka Father Divine Haasan) of the Colored American National Organization*

[CANO]; Stokely Delmar Hart, James Graves, and Annabelle Moore of the Brotherhood of Liberty for the Black People of America [BLBPA], and Frederick H. Hammurabi Robb of the Century Service Exchange."

Several days earlier, five members of the Ethiopian Pacific Movement [EPM] -- Robert O. Jordan (aka Leonard Robert Jordan), James Thornhill, Lester Holness, the Rev. Ralph Green Best, and Joseph Hartrey, an Irishman -- were indicted in New York City on the more serious charges. Less raucously, back in May, Ministers David X (aka David Jones and David Duvon) and Sultan Muhammad of the ATOI's Washington and Milwaukee temples, respectively, were detained on charges of sedition as well. In October the head of the International Reassemble of the Church of Freedom League, Inc. [IRCFL], the Rev. Ethelbert A. Broaster, was arrested in New Orleans.) The following January, a second round of indictments occurred in East St. Louis, where Bishop David D. Erwin and General Lee Butler, two leaders of the Pacific Movement of the Eastern World [PMEW], were also charged with crimes against the State. In Newark, seven members of the House of Israel [HOI] -- Brother Rueben Israel (aka Askew Thomas), Alfred Woods, Isaiah Cald, Robert Moses, Oscar Rumlin, Dawsey Johnson, and Jeremiah Ardis -- were seized as draft evaders.

This history that surrounds World War II is connected to today's events in several ways. First of all, laws such as the Espionage Act of 1917 and the Selective Training and Service Act of 1940 were used to imprison these courageous patriots that had emerged from the oppressed masses. Today we have the Patriot Act and the National Defense Authorization Act in place to legalize the same kind of wicked round up of Black Messianic Dissidents. Secondly the main ingredients of the World War II protest movement among Blacks was the message and influence of Master Fard Muhammad being carried by the Honorable Elijah Muhammad. He taught that the Japanese were the Brown brothers of the Black man of Africa and America. Today the main ingredient is the message and teaching of Master Fard Muhammad via the world wide ministry of the Honorable Minister Louis Farrakhan. Minister Farrakhan teaches that we are the brothers of the Muslim world and must not join in with the western powers to kill our Muslim brothers.

But those are social and political connections. There is also a religious and spiritual connection. Bruce Ritter writes in his article 7 Signs of A Falling Nation that *"In an interview with the Financial Times, U.S. Comptroller General David Walker stated that the United States government "is on a 'burning platform' of unsustainable policies and practices with fiscal deficits, chronic healthcare under funding, immigration, and overseas military commitments threatening a crisis if action is not taken soon…"*

The article added, "Mr. Walker warned that there were 'striking similarities' between America's current situation and the factors that brought down Rome, including 'declining moral values and political civility at home, an over-confident and over-extended military in foreign lands and fiscal irresponsibility by central government.'" General Walker's comparison of America to Ancient Rome is in agreement with author Cullen Murphy who wrote the book *The New Rome: The Fall of an Empire and the Fate of America*. In his book Murphy describes how Rome's imprint affected the known world in colossal ways as it exported its military, culture, art, architecture, clothes, and food. Murphy adds that Roman law and Roman moral values powerfully influenced and dominated the people under its sphere. This is also true of America's global influence and power.

The comparison of America to ancient Rome is important because the Bible's Messiah, Jesus, lived under Roman authority. And while religion has sought to limit Jesus' value to a role as the *"saviour from sin,"* many modern scholars like Dr. Obery T. Hendricks are drawn to Jesus the Revolutionary and thusly see him as a natural inspiration to modern social and political dissidents. Hendricks says Jesus the Revolutionary epitomizes and embodies messianic or God conscious dissent. Hendricks identifies some of the strategies of Jesus the Revolutionary by noting that *Jesus treated the people's needs as holy; Jesus also called the demons out by name; Jesus exposed the workings of Satan, and he gave a voice to the voiceless.*

Therefore American dissent must necessarily be of the messianic type because America's domination of the world results from her mastery of the trans-Atlantic slave trade. This commerce in Black bodies netted for America centuries of free labor and caused her to leap frog older nation-states very quickly en route to becoming the leading world superpower. Again, the messianic connection lies in America's reliance on slavery and the fact the same scenario of nations depending on slavery produced the Biblical Messiah to end it and call into judgment the slave holding nation that upheld it.

The question now is will America continue her punishment of Black Messianic Dissidents. Will she continue to frame mischief by means of law? Is Farrakhan in the cross-hairs? Are his followers to be imprisoned for supporting him in his criticism of America's unjust wars against the Muslim world? I guess for now we will have to wait and see.

10 Reasons to Support Minister Farrakhan's Presence On College Campuses

1. **Minister Farrakhan's Message of Self-Reliance is perfect for Black college students.** The *Chronicle of Higher Education* published an article, written by Ohio University professor of economics Richard Vedder, titled "Why Did 17 Million Students Go to College?" In this article Vedder documented all the Americans with high-level-education degrees that are either not working in their field or not working at all. *"Over 317,000 waiters and waitresses have college degrees (over 8,000 of them have doctoral or professional degrees), along with over 80,000 bartenders, and over 18,000 parking lot attendants. All told, some 17,000,000 Americans with college degrees are doing jobs that the BLS [Bureau of Labor Statistics] says require less than the skill levels associated with a bachelor's degree."* At least 5,057 PhDs are working as janitors. The Honorable Minister Louis Farrakhan's message is the antidote to this problem of students graduating from school and being unable to get a job commensurate with their skills, talents, abilities and education. Minister Farrakhan has long taught what a staple of NOI teachings is—that Black students should get an education that enables them to go into business, become entrepreneurs and be in a position to employ our own people. Jews do this all the time and they are successful.

2. **Minister Farrakhan teaches students to avoid the pitfalls of student loan debt. The Minister spoke recently at UC Berkeley, where students graduate with an average debt of $16,056, according to a recent NBC article written by Ayesha Minhaj.** The Honorable Minister Louis Farrakhan teaches that debt is slavery. The Nation of Islam has always taught Black people that we should be thrifty and spend and invest our money wisely. The Minister's message to the students will guide them into fields that will give them the greatest ROI or return on their investment of time, money and effort.

3. **The ban against Minister Farrakhan on college campuses is a weapon in the ongoing economic, political and social crucifixion of strong Black leadership.** *The Secret Relationship Between Blacks and Jews, Volume 2,* lists many who were victims of Jewish castigation and consequent economic retaliation only because they dared to critique Jewish behavior *and* venture into the arena of economic independence. (Malcolm X, Martin Luther King, Booker T. Washington, Oprah Winfrey, Julian Bond and Bishop Desmond Tutu et al have all been labeled at some point in their careers as "anti-Semitic.")
The paternalistic Jewish strategy for Black self-help—known as "non-economic liberalism"—was developed by the Jewish president and founder of the NAACP, Joel Spingarn. Spingarn and his Jewish and Gentile cohorts steered Blacks far away from the world of commerce and trade and banking and finance, even though, according to the *Universal Jewish Encyclopedia,* Jews "were pioneers in the primary stages of capitalist development and therefore held a dominant position in these cultural economic functions which may be called the nervous system of capitalist economy. Banking, the stock market, export and import fall within this classification." Joel Spingarn nonetheless advised W.E.B. Dubois and the NAACP to adopt the lame-duck strategy of "non-economic liberalism." This pointed avoidance of economics has made all our efforts in the fields of politics, education and law futile, because our activities lacked a collective economic component.

4. **Zionist criticism of Minister Farrakhan is unjustified. Raising the Minister's "words" to the level of "deeds" is an illogical fallacy.** It is especially irrational when you consider that Farrakhan's words have never harmed a Jewish man, woman or child. On the contrary, Jewish views of Blacks have had harmful effects all throughout history. For instance, the so-called Curse of Ham—a Jewish Talmudic invention—alleges all Blacks and Africans have been cursed Black by the God of Abraham. This myth permitted the Trans-Atlantic Slave Trade to be carried on with religious zeal and fervor. And the Jews were sophisticated masters in this trade in Black human cargo. According to Dr. Arnold Wiznitzer, Jews *"dominated*

the slave trade....The buyers who appeared at the auctions were almost always Jews, and because of this lack of competitors they could buy slaves at low prices." Slave trading, asserts Wiesenthal Center scholar Dr. Harold Brackman, "became a *'Jewish' mercantile specialty."* The *Jewish Encyclopedia* adds that "Jewish commercial activity" included a "monopoly of the slave trade." In fact, a Jewish shipper had a monopoly on trade to the notorious slave dungeon at Gorée Island—the Auschwitz of the Black Holocaust. Dr. Rabbi Bertram Korn unequivocally stated: *"It would seem to be realistic to conclude that any Jew who could afford to own slaves and had need for their services would do so....Jews participated in every aspect and process of the exploitation of the defenseless blacks."*

5. **Blacks must be encouraged to unite as Jews and other ethnic groups in America have done.** Minister Farrakhan encourages cooperation, brotherhood and operational unity in his message to the students. The idea of unity is a strong theme in the religion of Islam. Eugenicist and racist Lothrop Stoddard, quoting British naval officer Charles Elliott, wrote in *The Rising Tide of Color Against White World Supremacy* that Islam "can still give [the Black Africans] ... a unity of which they are otherwise incapable."

6. **Black youth of today are largely viewed as incorrigible. The source of influence for today's youth comes primarily from the Hip-Hop culture.** And it is Minister Farrakhan who is the godfather of the Hip-Hop culture, as his 10-year New York ministry helped birth the popular youth culture in the Bronx in 1972. Hip-Hop bears the imprint of Minister Farrakhan, for it is a hybrid art form combining spoken word, musical accompaniment and performance art. Minister Farrakhan's public life reveals a devotion to the spoken word of truth and a musical virtuosity, as demonstrated by his mastery of the violin and concert performance. His connection to the Hip-Hop community automatically grants him entry to our youth's hearts and minds.

7. **Jewish Groups attack Farrakhan but the Nation of Islam teachings are laced with concepts familiar and agreeable to Jews.** The Nation of Islam agrees with Jews that education, economic autonomy, marriage and family, ethnic loyalty, knowledge sharing and a disciplined personal life make communities strong and constitute the path to power. The Minister's message, therefore, if internalized by the students, becomes an equalizing force propelling the Black students from ignominy and poverty to honor and abundance, thus enabling them to share company with Jews and other members of the human family that are successful—not only in business, but in all areas of life.

8. **Minister Farrakhan's spirit of revolutionary defiance is necessarily contagious.** Jesus, Muhammad, Martin Luther King Jr., Marcus Garvey and the great "change agents" of history never compromised truth and principle to avoid controversy. They all were known for "speaking truth to power." If the students internalize this spirit, they will become what the Black people of America need of a "new intelligentsia" that is passionate, principled, purified and prepared to lead our people toward a full and complete freedom.

9. **There is a need for an Anti-War Movement among Black Students.** Black, Latino and poor White youth make up the U. S. armed forces. They will be the casualties in America's projected war with Iran. America's foreign policies are influenced by the greedy multi-national corporations whose desire is to control and capitalize on the precious natural resources of other countries. These are the same corporations that enjoy close relationships with the banks that become rich through student-loan debt. It is no accident that often the only opportunity for forgiveness of student loan debt comes in the guise of a military offer to repay student loans if they join the armed forces. The voice of Minister Farrakhan, like that of his teacher the Honorable Elijah Muhammad, warns the students not to join the U.S. government's war effort in the Muslim world. Minister Farrakhan condemns America's long history of using the poor to fight the wars of the rich, and his message to the students is that they should be conscientious objectors.

10. **Minister Farrakhan awakens the students to their divine destiny.** Every generation must make its mark on history. Black youth are the descendants of the Africans brought to America to be made slaves. That experience of enslavement has a scriptural and religious parallel: the Biblical and Quranic narratives of the enslavement of the Children of Israel. According to both Scriptures, it was the youth of the wandering Children of Israel who forged the way for their entire people to inhabit God's Promised Land. It was the youth, led by Joshua and Caleb, who were unafraid of and conquered the "giants" in that land and were consequently dubbed the "Joshua Generation." Minister Farrakhan teaches that Black youth are indeed the Joshua Generation for our people. His message is the inspirational food that Black youth need to see themselves as this new generation of fearless leaders.

Is Help for Blacks, Hurt for Jews?

The Anti-Black world-view of Neil Steinberg

On September 30 Neil Steinberg released the latest propaganda attack on the Honorable Minister Louis Farrakhan and the Nation of Islam. His poisonous and uninformed article has created a teachable moment. I don't know if Steinberg is willing to learn, but I am definitely willing to teach.

His attack is strategically timed to be distributed in the immediate aftermath of Minister Farrakhan's wonderfully successful tour of New York City for the promotion of peace and an end to gun violence. Black people should, by now, begin to notice that whenever strong and uncompromising voices of Black self-help and determination begin to make progress, Zionist Jewish forces emerge to attack them. Any Black person that reads his rants against Minister Farrakhan must understand the lens through which Steinberg views the Minister and all Black people, for that matter.

Steinberg's lens is apparently the Babylonian Talmud, which is a commentary on the Torah (Old Testament) written by early Jewish Rabbis. The Talmud says that Blacks are cursed by God to be servants to Jews and that Blacks are deemed to only have value as servants of Jews. Dr. Harold Brackman of the Simon Wiesenthal Center wrote in his doctoral dissertation that Jewish Rabbis created the myth of the Curse of Ham, *"There is no denying that the Babylonian Talmud was the first source to read a Negrophobic content into the [Noahic] episode by stressing Canaan's fraternal connection with Cush... The more important version of the myth, however, ingeniously ties in the origins of blackness — and of other, real and imagined Negroid traits — with Noah's Curse itself."* This anti-Black worldview has been on display as recently as 2005, when the head of the Shas's Council of Torah Sages in Israel, Rabbi Ovadia Yosef, said that God sent Hurricane Katrina to destroy New Orleans because Blacks live there and were not studying enough Torah!

Moses Maimonides, who is called by the *Encyclopedia of the Jewish Religion* "the symbol of the pure and orthodox faith," wrote in his *Guide to the Perplexed*: *"...the Negroes found in the remote South, and those who resemble them from among them that are with us in these climes. The status* of those is like that of irrational animals. To my mind they do not have the rank of men, but have among the beings a rank lower than the rank of man but higher than the rank of apes. For they have the external shape and lineaments of a man and a faculty of discernment that is superior to that of the apes."

This is the lens through which Neil Steinberg views Black people. This is what Minister Farrakhan and all strong Black leaders in our history have had to fight. These anti-Black ideas have garnered wide acceptance even within the ranks of our own people. The poetess Phyllis Wheatley wrote of her color as being a *"diabolic dye."* The slave Jupiter Hammond is an example of the great harm the Hamitic myth has had upon the minds of Black slaves. He rebuked Blacks who earnestly desired freedom with these words: *"It may seem hard for us if we think our masters wrong in holding us slaves to obey in all things, but who of us dare dispute with God! He has commanded us to obey, and we ought to do it cheerfully and freely....for my own part I do not wish to be free; for many of us who are grown up slaves have always had masters to take care of themselves; and it may be for our own comfort to remain as we are."*

So if Blacks are cursed with Blackness and if Black people's only purpose in life is to be a servant to the Jews, then any and all persons who seek to secure for Black people a different and more ennobled destiny must be attacked. This is why Steinberg and his ilk are busy demonizing the Honorable Marcus Mosiah Garvey and the Honorable Minister Louis Farrakhan. Minister Farrakhan and Marcus Garvey are exponents of what is called Black Nationalism. And it is really Black Nationalism that Steinberg wants to equate with anti-Semitism.

But what is Black Nationalism? Nationalism, according to Dr. Molefi Kete Asante, *"is a relationship among people with a common heritage and with common expectations. Land acquisition is merely the ultimate stage of nationalism. The consummation and crystallization of our aspirations into an organic and systemic instrument for emancipatory politics is the first objective of systematic nationalism. This process is accomplished through historically and culturally determined actions for national expression. It contradicts attempts at national oppression through the exploitative uses of culture, science, religion, and economics. Emancipatory politics is the keystone of nationalistic struggle. It liberates the mind from the duality of marginal existence. Nationalists are therefore capable of functioning in any situation. What is necessary, absolutely necessary, is an attachment to the national idea...The correctness of systematic nationalism stems from its assault on the twin evils of race and class exploitation. This, however, is not its philosophical grounding; it is rather its activist character."*

I don't know any Black person that wouldn't want this. In fact, I don't know any Jewish person that would disagree with such an ideology. Black Nationalism actually mirrors what Jews have done to secure themselves. They have land, dual citizenship with Israel, economic strength and its resulting political strength. Jews are respected and admired for their economic strength, unity, culture and values concerning education and family life. The Black Nationalist view is that Black people deserve the same, yet our Jewish friends never steered us in that direction.

Joel Spingarn and the Jewish leaders of the NAACP directed Blacks to do the very opposite of what Jews do to become successful in society. So the NAACP and most in the Civil Rights Movement adopted the philosophy Spingarn termed "non-economic liberalism"—which encouraged and fostered a beggar's mentality in Blacks. It suggested that what Blacks desired and deserved of justice, equality and an overall better quality of life could only be achieved through picketing, marching and begging the government. This was never the model that Jews themselves employed. They developed strength through unity, self-love, entrepreneurship, and the establishment of Jewish enclaves all over America. These are the tenets that Brother Marcus Garvey, the Honorable Elijah Muhammad and Minister Farrakhan have promoted for Black people.

Steinberg asked, "Where has Minister Farrakhan led his Nation?" I ask Mr. Steinberg, Where have Jews led Blacks? If the Jews' involvement was so beneficial to the Black struggle, why isn't the Black condition equal to the Jewish condition? Why don't we hear of the plight of the Jewish male like there is a plight of the Black male? Why is there no Jew-on-Jew crime and violence like there is a Black-on-Black crime problem? I have yet to hear of a Jewish HIV epidemic like the Black HIV epidemic statistics trumpet. And the prison industrial complex appears to have no adverse effects on the Jewish community. It is clear that Jewish paternalism concerning Black issues is for the purpose of sabotage and not salvation. It is clear that Blacks have not been given the secret to the Jewish Phenomenon of success within American society.

Instead, Steinberg and the Zionist lobby are content to fight any strong and courageous Black person who seeks to help Black people out of the miserable condition of slavery, suffering and death. *The Secret Relationship between Blacks and Jews, Volume 2,* contains a shocking list of Blacks that have at various times in their careers been labeled anti-Semites. Their only crime was advocating a position of Black self-help, an act viewed by Jews as being hurtful to Jewish interests.

Booker T. Washington	W.E.B. DuBois
Marcus Garvey	Martin L. King Jr.
Malcolm X	Hon. Elijah Muhammad
Pres. Nelson Mandela	Bishop Desmond Tutu
Julian Bond	Kwame Ture
Andrew Young	Kweisi Mfume
Rev. Al Sharpton	Rev. Jesse Jackson
Rev. Joseph Lowery	J.A. Rogers
James Baldwin	Richard Wright
Julius Lester	Alice Walker
Michael Jackson	Spike Lee
Ice Cube	Arsenio Hall
Muhammad Ali	Public Enemy
Oprah Winfrey	John Hope Franklin

What Steinberg fears is the wide acceptance of the Honorable Minister Louis Farrakhan by the masses of Black people. He had hoped that the Black masses had bought in to the notion of a "post-racial" America. He had expected that the election of a Black President of the United States of America would extinguish the light of Black people's desire for freedom, justice and equality. Steinberg's dream is that the Black community remains deprived of self-determination, unity and economic power. What Steinberg really wanted to write was how dumbfounded he is over the tenacity, durability and wide reach of the leadership of Minister Farrakhan. For it is the leadership of Minister Farrakhan that the masses of Black people now see as a torchlight, amid an ever-increasing darkness inside America.

Did Minister Louis Farrakhan Give Birth to Hip-Hop?

"Environment shapes heredity." Hon. Elijah Muhammad

The Scholars on the Origin of Rap/Hip Hop Music

Rap music has had a profound impact on the African American community in the United States. Its greatest significance, to my mind, derives from the fact that it has fostered a profound nationalism in the youth of Black America. Arguably, hip-hop has become a conduit for African American culture to a greater extent than even jazz. Where the latter could, through its polyrhythmic syncopations, embrace both the nuances and jagged edges of the collective Black experience, it could not self-consciously energize the nationalist ethos in quite the way the more lyrically focused hip-hop does.

Hip-hop, or rap music, began in the early 1970s. The first synthesis of self-conscious poetry and music can be traced, most directly, to the Black Nationalist Last Poets. Their albums The Last Poets, Chastisement, This is Madness, and others have become classics in the African American community. When one member who separated from the group, with the stage name "Lightning Rod," used a musical score provided by Kool & The Gang as a backdrop to his lyrical narrative of a day in the life of two hustlers, he had no idea he was laying the basis for an entirely new musical genre. This album, Hustler's Convention, was a mainstay in the album collection of a South Bronx DJ named Kool Herc. Almost to a person, it is agreed that hip-hop began with Kool Herc. **–Errol A. Henderson, Black Nationalism and Rap Music**

As the limitations of electoral politics became glaringly and painfully apparent to the post-civil rights generation, rap artists idolized the words and works of political personalities such as Marcus Garvey, Malcolm X, and Louis Farrakhan, men whose uncompromising public personae and urban, poor/working-class roots stood as an example to those young black men whose status was undermined in the postindustrial capitalist economy. "God knows, when I heard Farrakhan, I had never heard a black man talk like that. It blew my mind, absolutely blew my mind," Hip Hop journalist/activist

Kevin Powell recalled of his introduction to Farrakhan during the mid-1980s. "It was intoxicating, as intoxicating as crack was for a lot of people in our community in the '80s."

-Charise Cheney, "Revolutionary Generation": (En) gendering the Golden Age of Rap Nationalism

The Nation of Islam is generally acknowledged as having a deep influence on rap music. Rappers such as Poor Righteous Teachers, King Sun, Brand Nubian, Movement Ex, and Public Enemy, frequently quote and draw inspiration from the Honorable Elijah Muhammad (founder of the Nation of Islam), Malcolm X, and Minister Louis Farrakhan. The famed boxer, Muhammad Ali, was also an early rapper.

-Catherine Tabb Powell, Rap Music: An Education with a Beat from the Street

Musician Grandmaster Flash defined hip hop as "the only genre of music that allows us to talk about almost anything. Musically, it allows us to sample and play and create poetry to the beat of the music. It's highly controversial, but that's the way the game is." Hip hop culture began in the 1970s in the Bronx, N.Y., among African-American, Latino, and Caribbean youth who created intercultural crews ("new kinds of families") of MCs/rappers, disc jockeys, break dancers, and graffiti artists whose art and style expressed resistance to postindustrial conditions and the destruction of jobs, affordable housing, and support systems in working-class black and Latino neighborhoods at the beginning of the Ronald Reagan-George H.W. Bush era.

-Professor Richard Brent Turner, The Influence of Malcolm X and Martin Luther King Jr. on Hip Hop

The real significance of hip-hop is not, however related to those rappers(amoral and obscene), but rather to the religio-politically oriented "message rap" artists, who have steadily found success since the mid-1980s....The Hip-Hop movement's role in popularizing the message of Black militant Islam cannot be overestimated. What reggae was to Rastafarianism in the 70's...Hip Hop is to the spread of Black Islam in the 80's and 90's....Expressing thanks and support for the Nation of Islam and Louis

Farrakhan has become almost standard practice on the rap albums, and long quotations from NOI literature are often included in the lyrics

-Professor Mattias Gardell, In The Name of Elijah Muhammad Louis Farrakhan and The Nation of Islam

Connecting The Dots on Minister Farrakhan's Presence At Hip Hop's Genesis

Hip Hop Born in New York circa 1972-All scholars and students of Hip Hop history agree that this musical art form began in the early 1970s in New York City. The Honorable Minister Louis Farrakhan was then the Minister of Temple No.7 in New York. His influence was transmitted to all of the Black citizens of New York via his 5,000 followers and his 18 satellite Temples of Islam. The Minister was also being heard on the radio 6 times per week. Such a wide and far reaching presence easily made him one of the most influential forces in all of New York City. This is important when you consider that environment shapes heredity. Minister Farrakhan's ministry was saturating the collective consciousness of Black and Hispanic New Yorkers with the revolutionary message found within the teachings of the Most Honorable Elijah Muhammad.

The Presence of Caribbean DJs help start the music- New York has long been a haven for Caribbean immigrants. Minister Farrakhan is connected to the Caribbean peoples through his parentage; his mother being from the Island of Nevis and his father being from Jamaica. The Minister has spoken often in the Islands and received warmly as a native son and head of state.

Hip Hop as hybrid of spoken word and performance art- Hip Hop is a unique and attractive art form. It is a hybrid or mixture of spoken word, performance art and musicianship. In this way it bears the definite imprint of the Farrakhan influence. For it is Minister Farrakhan's professional career where he has demonstrated mastery in both spoken word-as the towering figure known quite simply as The Minister- and musicianship-where he has performed and still plays classical violin. Hip Hop is Minister Farrakhan's baby. Rappers to this day pay homage to him and see him as the peacemaker and strong man for Black people.

Hip Hop As Music With A Message-As Professor Mattias Gardell points out Hip Hop begins as 'message rap.' Throughout the history of hip hop artists have written lyrics to include urban social commentary, revolutionary manifestos and homage to the giants of the Black liberation struggle. This characteristic of the Hip Hop culture is directly reflective of the ministry of the Honorable Minister Louis Farrakhan. Public Enemy's Chuck D once wrote "Farrakhan's a prophet that I think you ought to listen to, what he can say to you, what you ought to do, is follow for now…" Hip Hop's revolutionary, truth to power quality is more evidence of the influential role of Minister Louis Farrakhan. His mighty ministry in New York City during the 1970's created a unique climate in New York where cultural, educational and artistic trends were born. To that end we consider the Honorable Minister Louis Farrakhan the Godfather of the Hip Hop cultural phenomenon.

God Gives The Minister A Vision of Things To Come

Proof of a Vision: The Honorable Minister Louis Farrakhan's MESSAGE from Elijah By Tingba Muhammad, NOI Research Group

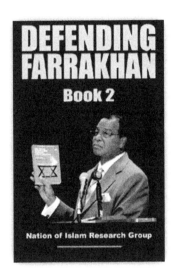

The vision-like experience that The Honorable Minister Louis Farrakhan had in 1985 is part of the instructional fabric of the Nation of Islam. Now there is conclusive supporting data discovered by the NOI Research Group that establish the factual basis for The Minister's spiritual experience. This body of data shows a flurry of secret diplomatic and military activity at the moments in time in which The Minister says his vision-like experience occurred. This evidence is drawn from, among other sources, now-declassified documents, new investigative journalism, White House records, and diary entries of the President of the United States. There is even a photograph that has been found of the very meeting in question.

Minister Farrakhan describes the event as a "more than a vision experience" and the fullness of that seminal event was catalogued in Mother Tynetta Muhammad's insightful book *The Comer by Night* and in a series of articles authored by Bro. Jabril Muhammad that appeared in the *Final Call* newspaper. Our research will address the portion of Min. Farrakhan's September 17, 1985, experience that is quoted below:

> "In this vision...Elijah Muhammad spoke to me these words: *'President Reagan has met with his joint chiefs of staff to plan a war. I want you to hold a press conference and make known their plans. And tell them that you got it from me, Elijah Muhammad, on The Wheel.'...*"

The reference to *The Wheel* is highly significant in the Teachings of the Nation of Islam in that it refers to the "wheel-shaped plane known as the Mother of (all) Planes"—"a masterpiece of mechanics"—a human-built plane spanning "a half-mile by a half-mile." Launched in 1929, it was built by the man known to believers as Allah in Person, Master Fard Muhammad, the long-awaited "Messiah" of the Christians and the "Mahdi" of the Muslims. This awe-inspiring "Mother Plane" houses 1,500 smaller "baby planes," and whereas the Nation of Islam has clearly identified these aircraft, when they are seen by the general public they are referred to as UFOs. The Bible refers to these vehicles in its Book of Ezekiel (1:16) and in Exodus (13:21) as "the wheel(s)" and "a cloud by day and a pillar of fire by night."

According to the Hon. Elijah Muhammad through his Representative Minister Farrakhan, The Wheel is "a weapon that all of the technology of the Western White world can't fathom," whose purpose is to destroy the present world. So the appearance of Elijah on that Wheel in Minister Farrakhan's vision carries a great significance—and not just for Nation of Islam members and believers. This Wheel would have intrigued Ronald Reagan himself, for in 1974 he claimed to have had an encounter with a UFO while he was still governor of California. A week later he described the event to Norman C. Miller, then Washington bureau chief for the *Wall Street Journal*:

> "I was in a plane last week when I looked out the window and saw this white light. It was zigzagging around. I went up to the pilot and said, 'Have you seen anything like that before?' He was shocked and said, 'Nope.' And I said to him: 'Let's follow it!' We followed it for several minutes. It was a bright white light. We followed it to Bakersfield, and all of a sudden to our utter amazement it went straight up into the heavens. When we got off the plane, I told Nancy all about it."

The pilot of Governor Reagan's plane, retired U.S. Air Force Colonel Bill Paynter, backed up Reagan's version of the incident with the UFO:

> "It appeared to be several hundred yards away. It was a fairly steady light until it began to accelerate, then it appeared to elongate. The light took off....The UFO went from a normal cruise speed to a fantastic speed instantly....We didn't file a report on the object because for a

long time they considered you a nut if you saw a UFO."

Reagan's deep fascination with this issue is demonstrated at various points in his life and so the emphatic point made by The Messenger—**"And tell them that you got it from me, Elijah Muhammad, on The Wheel"**—may have been meant specifically for Reagan to hear. And Reagan's "close encounter" was carefully concealed by the media and his handlers until after he left the White House, so Minister Farrakhan *could not have known about Reagan's experience with The Wheel* through any conventional means.

During a press conference he held in February of 1986, it dawned on The Minister that his vision of the Reagan-planned war was in fact targeting the North African nation of Libya and its leader, Col. Muammar Gadhafi. Two months later, on April 16, 1986, Pres. Reagan did indeed attack Libya—almost seven months to the day from the Minister's September 17th experience.

What actually was happening in the Reagan White House and in the United States military during those critical months in time that correspond to The Minister's profound experience on The Wheel?

First let us consider the strategic role of Libya in world affairs that made it a target of the world's most powerful nation. It must here be remembered that Reagan was described as being "obsessed" with Libya and its leader throughout his presidency (1981–1989). Not only was Col. Gadhafi sitting on massive strategic oil reserves, but he was seeking to unite all Arab, Muslim, and African oil states, and, more troubling, he was governing a large part of Chad, which is a major producer of uranium. Gadhafi's Soviet-assisted vision for the region was diametrically opposed to the colonization schemes of the West and its Israeli representatives. And Reagan's obsession had been an American obsession from the nation's very beginning. Tripoli was the center of the first covert operation in American history—under Pres. Thomas Jefferson in 1804—and it was now the concern of the Reaganites.

The Reagan administration had been aware and approving of a 1984 assassination attempt against Gadhafi by French agents that failed. And secretly, the United States was engaged with Israel and its Arab client states in a propaganda operation that not only planted false stories in the media to link Libya with *any* "terrorist" act—bombings, kidnappings, hijackings, assassinations, etc.—but also invented the "evidence" that "implicated" Libya. Records now show that operatives of the Central Intelligence Agency (CIA) and the Israeli Mossad performed terrorist acts and blamed Libya. This, the Reaganites hoped, would turn Col. Gadhafi into a pariah, which would justify his violent removal.

In the months leading up to Minister Farrakhan's experience, evidence shows a series of political crises that foreshadowed the early September 1985 meetings of high-level military officials in the Reagan administration.

Though Reagan's published diary was clearly edited to be made compatible with official American propaganda, he demonstrates "concern" over Libya in several pre-September entries. On June 27, 1985, Reagan mentions that *"Gadhafi is talking to about a joint terrorist war against us."* On July 3: *"We are also discussing Iran & Syria a plan to take care of the Libya situation— including bombing some known terrorist training centers."* Records of the National Security Council (the body responsible for national security issues) almost mirror Reagan's diary. They similarly show that Libya was the topic of their meetings on June 25th and July 3rd. In a July 9 speech, Pres. Reagan used his most aggressive rhetoric against "a confederation of terrorist states" he identified as Nicaragua, Libya, North Korea, Cuba, and Iran. They were, he said, "the strangest collection of misfits, Looney Tunes and squalid criminals since the advent of the Third Reich"—a malicious reference designed for Israeli ears.

Then, according to journalist Bob Woodward, an emergency meeting was called in mid-July when state department officials overseas were secretly flown home to—in their words—"stop the madmen in the White House" who wanted an immediate war against Libya. For the moment they were successful.

Between July and September of 1985 plans were developed for a joint US–Egyptian military offensive against Libya, but it was rejected only because Egypt's Pres. Mubarak did not trust the United States. The plan was dubbed "Operation Flower," with its two components called "Operation Tulip" and

"Operation Rose." Both were covert CIA operations, with "Tulip" using Libyan exiles to overthrow Gadhafi in a *coup d'état*, and "Rose" being a joint U.S.–Egyptian military campaign against the Libyan government. On September 1st, units of the Libyan military did in fact try to overthrow Gadhafi, but the rebellion was crushed and 43 senior officers were arrested.

The Meetings

Minister Farrakhan's September 17th vision referred to meeting(s) of the Joint Chiefs of Staff (JCS) earlier that month. Based on the best evidence, the secret meeting(s) probably occurred on September 3rd, two days after the failed *coup d'état* in Libya, and then again on September 9th during a secret gathering of top military leaders from nations in alliance with the United States (NATO). The latter meeting is depicted in a photograph now held at the Reagan Library (see below).

Figure 1. September 9, 1985, meeting with NATO commanders. Could this be the meeting Minister Farrakhan was told of on The WHEEL?

On **September 3rd**, returning from vacation, Pres. Reagan met with his National Security Council, and it's Planning Group. According to Reagan's diary, *"[Egyptian] Pres. Mubarak believes Gadhafi of Libya is a threat to all the N. African countries & mainly Egypt. We've been meeting with [him] on how we can assist him if Egypt is attacked. Do we all go out & join in a war & would our people support such a move? There is no doubt Egypt & the Suez Canal are very important to our security. Still it's a complex problem. For now we'll keep on studying contingency plans with Pres. Mubarak."*

Six days later, on **September 9th**, Reagan writes: *"I welcomed the 18 Generals commanding their country's forces in NATO. They are here visiting our military bases."*

That language suggesting that the "visit" was ceremonial in nature was clearly for public consumption, but it is evident that wars were being planned and various military roles were being assigned. The "visit" of these top commanding generals is not like a convention or annual gathering. If it were ceremonial, there would be plenty of photo opportunities and chest-pounding for the non-NATO world to see—much like the Russians' annual review of their weaponry through Red Square. But the media make no mention of this extraordinary meeting (or their "visiting military bases"). Nor does Reagan say when these commanders arrived in the United States and when they departed.

If, as Reagan says, "the 18 generals" are "visit military bases"–*plural*–one must realize there are over 500 bases in America alone, and dozens of military facilities in the area surrounding Washington, DC. Their visit to the United States, some from thousands of miles away, must have been for at least several days. And it is highly unlikely that eighteen NATO commanders would come to America and not meet with the Joint Chiefs of Staff, which is made up of the top commanders of the U.S. Navy, Army, Marines, and Air Force.

This was *most likely* the meeting that The Honorable Minister Louis Farrakhan was told of on The Wheel. And it is clear that The Minister *could not have known* of it through any conventional means.

Later that day (September 9th), Reagan meets with a group of Jewish leaders for a "photo op," but with the Middle East on the brink of war the description of this meeting as *ceremonial* is suspect. At about this time the Israeli Army was placed on heightened alert on at least five separate occasions.

The March to War

Immediately following those two (or more) planning meetings, a series of events occurred that continued the march toward the April 1986 bombing of Libya.

On **September 10**, Israel released the last of hundreds of Palestinians they held, whose freedom had been the stated motive for many of the Arab "terrorist" acts against Western targets. This preemptive move is clearly made by Israel at the behest of Reagan to eliminate any righteous grievances so that the planned war against Libya can proceed as a "retaliation" rather than as an unjustified act of aggression. On **September 11th**, another suspect 20-member delegation from the American Jewish Congress goes on a "fact-finding mission" to the Middle East. On **October 18th**, Operation Ghost Rider—a full rehearsal for a strike against Libya—commenced in Newfoundland, Canada.

A bombing incident on **December 27th** at the Rome and Vienna airports kills 20 people and 5 Americans and accelerates the White House rhetoric. On **Jan 7th** Reagan blames the incident on Gadhafi, and now the die is cast and the American "retaliation" is assured.

In February 1986, it crystallizes for Minister Louis Farrakhan that the war he was told of was indeed to be launched against Libya. As he recounts: *"From Tripoli, speaking before the representatives of approximately 80 nations, I told the vision publicly, sending back to the United States a warning to President Reagan and Secretary of State George Schultz."*

On April 14, 1986, Ronald Reagan ordered a strike on five targets in Libya. And on the next day 33 attack aircraft struck Tripoli. The total number of Libyans murdered in the attack were estimated at 60, including Col. Gadhafi's recently adopted infant daughter Hana. Far more innocents may have perished, including the leader himself, *had not Minister Farrakhan relayed that divine warning*—from *The Wheel*.

Reagan boasted that "If necessary, we shall do it again." Under President Barack Hussein Obama, they did.

The Honorable Minister Louis Farrakhan's
Vision-like Experience on The Wheel: Timeline

Hon. Elijah Muhammad: "President Reagan has met with the Joint Chiefs of Staff to plan a war."

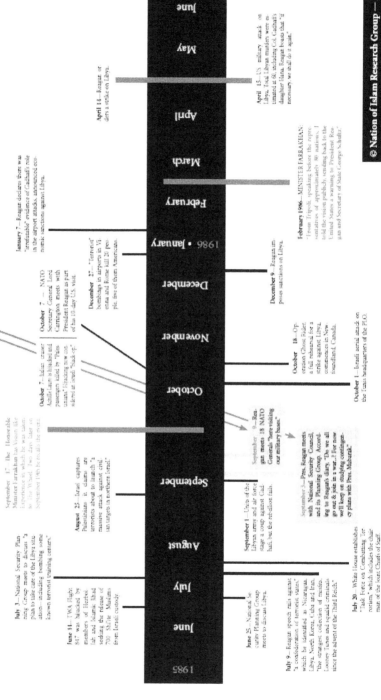

Farrakhan plays Mendelssohn

By Debra Hanania-Freeman and Fred Haight

In 1993, the Honorable Minister Louis Farrakhan, the leader of the Nation of Islam, astonished the world with a virtuoso performance of one of the most

tender and compassionate pieces of music in the Classical repertoire, Felix Mendelssohn's Violin Concerto in E minor, Opus 64. The recently released videotape "For Love of Music-Farrakhan Plays the Violin" not only features the historic May 1993 concert, but also gives viewers an inside look at how and why that concert came to be. While there is no question that Farrakhan's startling solo performance, accompanied by the New World Orchestra conducted by Michael Morgan, is the high point of the videotape, it is also true that, as a totality, the complete production is an artful composition. In the introductory moments, we learn that Louis Farrakhan's love of the violin and Classical music is not new or casual, but an art form he has been committed to for over fifty years. We also learn, through the words of his son Mustapha, that although circumstances had forced Farrakhan's formal training to cease some forty-four years prior to his 1993 performance, music was always very much part of his life.

Mustapha remembers a household in which he and his eight brothers and sisters were wakened to the sounds of their father's violin. Despite Farrakhan's obvious love of the instrument, the fact that he did not play publicly for some four decades was also a personal decision. At first, the young Louis Walcott was forced to abandon his formal training when he left his home in Boston to attend college in the South, where there were no Classical teachers for young blacks. In 1955, when Louis Walcott meets Elijah Muhammad for the first time, he responds to Muhammad's plea that his followers choose between entertainment and religion. It was Muhammad's view that the black people in America had enough entertainers and athletes, but were in desperate need of thinkers. Louis Walcott, soon to be Louis Farrakhan, dedicated himself to becoming a thinker and, at least for a while, put away his beloved instrument. By 1989, when the Mosque Maryam was dedicated in Chicago, Farrakhan had risen to lead the Nation of Islam, and was, depending on who was doing the talking, the most respected or most feared black leader in America. At the dedication of the mosque, Sylvia Olden Lee , a pianist and teacher of international stature (the first African-American professional musician at the New York Metropolitan Opera, where she was Vocal Coach 1954-56, and professor of vocal interpretation at the Curtis Institute of Music for more than 20 years), accompanied a fine young singer. We learn that afterwards, at a dinner at the minister's home, a string quartet played. Mrs. Lee reports that, obviously inspired by the day's events, when someone handed Farrakhan his violin, he rose to perform. Lee admits that she didn't expect much. "But," she reports, "I was absolutely startled. His performance was captivating; brilliant; prestissimos flying as he made his instrument sing along." She was so impressed, in fact, that she began to tell others. Among those she spoke to was Dr. Willis Patterson, Dean of the University of Michigan School of Music, and then head of the National Association of Negro Musicians. She asked him if he had a celebrity performer for the association's upcoming conference. When he said he did not, she suggested he invite Louis Farrakhan. Patterson was shocked. "Can he play?" he asked her. Sylvia Lee replied, "Oh, he can play; he plays like Isaac Stern." An invitation was sent and accepted. Minister Farrakhan played the Massenet "Meditation from Thais," but the idea of performing the piece he was learning when his formal training had ended-the Mendelssohn Concerto-was born.

Minister Farrakhan wanted to play it as a gift that he would give to others for his own sixtieth birthday. Having only learned the first movement of the three-movement piece, Farrakhan dedicated the next two years of his life to studying and perfecting it. During those two years, only those closest to him knew of his plan. He did not alter his grueling travel and speaking schedule. In fact, it was during this period that Louis

Farrakhan spoke in every major city in the United States with the goal of reaching 1 million black men. Yet he found the hours he needed to practice and to study. His teacher, a Russian Jewish concert artist by the name of Elaine Skorodin Fohrman, often accompanied him. Some of Louis Farrakhan's critics claimed that he selected a piece by Mendelssohn, a Jewish composer, as a cheap trick to cover his alleged anti-Semitism. , But when his son Mustapha is asked why Mendelssohn, he looks surprised. "Why Mendelssohn? It had to be Mendelssohn. He loved him."

The rest of the videotape tells a beautiful story of everything that went into the preparation of the concert. Minister Farrakhan's dedication to the music is only part of the story. We learn that an entire community had to mobilize to see the concert realized. A great deal of fear and slander and prejudice had to be overcome. Just before we are taken to the performance, Farrakhan tries to explain his motivation in taking on this task. He tells us, "Music, like truth, is the essence of my life. When I put down my violin to dedicate myself to my people, some of my thinking became narrow and nationalistic. But music expands my breast and I can feel not only the pain of my own people, but all of humanity. Its universality teaches of the beauty of all human beings. "He talks about how the human heart, like a fine instrument, can be crafted through the beauty of music to clear away ignorance and "lift men from where they are to where God wants them to be. People don't know Farrakhan; they don't know the soul of the man. I'd like them to. "On his choice of Mendelssohn, Farrakhan says, "The man's music was simply divine." But what of Farrakhan's music? By this time in the video, the viewer has no doubt of the nobility of the man or the mission, despite the venomous slanders that accompany nearly every mention of his name in print. The desire to use beautiful music to heal wounds, to open doors, especially for young people who might otherwise never be exposed to an orchestral Classical performance, has to do some good. But, we also know that the Mendelssohn piece remains out of reach to even some professionals. The bowing is very complex. The piece leaps from the lowest note to the highest; there are trills; double stops; all in quick succession. Well, we think, even a tiny step in the right direction is better than nothing. Finally, we arrive at the doors of Chicago's Christ Universal Temple. It is time for the concert.

But can Farrakhan play? To quote the New York Times critic (something we almost never do in this publication), "Can Louis Farrakhan play the violin? God bless us! He certainly can." First, a word on the composition. In most Classical concertos, there is a pause between the three movements. But, in this concerto, taking a cue from the late Beethoven , Mendelssohn links all three movements together without a break, indicating that he had a strong idea of the work as an integrated whole. Farrakhan clearly comprehends Mendelssohn's intent, and succeeds admirably in developing such a concept of this work. For example, the first movement of the Concerto is indicated "Allegro" (fast) and the third movement "Allegro molto vivace" (fast and very full of life). Although the emphasis "molto vivace" does not necessarily imply faster than simple "Allegro," violinists always play it very quickly, rather than think about what the indication actually means. The result is that although the third movement of the piece is joyous, in most recorded performances, the passion of the previous movements dissipates. The movement is usually only half as long as the first and tends to become a bit fluffy and light. Farrakhan takes the movement at a slower pace, allowing it to retain its jubilancy without becoming unserious. The listener hears the echoes of the first movement in his mind's ear, just as the composer intended. (Indeed, the transition from the second to the third, an "Allegretto ma non troppo" quotes from the first movement in order to underline the link.) Maestro Michael Morgan comments earlier in the video

that it is in the second movement that Louis Farrakhan's character comes out. A very interesting thing happens.

Maestro Morgan begins the movement in the slow, Adagio- like tempo in which it is usually played. When the violin enters, Farrakhan speeds up to the Andante (walking pace) which Mendelssohn himself indicated. We see Morgan turn his head with a puzzled look before he adjusts to the soloist's tempo. This is a cantabile (singing) movement. The traditional slower tempo allows a violinist to show how well he can make his instrument sing. But the Andante tempo taken by Farrakhan, with his instrument still singing beautifully, keeps a certain edge of tension coming out of the first movement and leading into the third. The concept of the work as a whole is developed, and a respect for its seriousness maintained. Farrakhan's ability to make his instrument sing deserves attention. All good instrumental music is based on the human voice and Minister Farrakhan has the mastery of bowing technique necessary to organize phrasing as he desires. But, there is also something more.

When Minister Farrakhan addresses the audience at the conclusion of his triumphant performance, he speaks of the fact that in music, every note has a different vibration; just as every human being "vibrates" differently. He jokes that the warm-up of any orchestra sounds like pure chaos-until the oboist plays the "A" to which the orchestra tunes. But, he emphasizes, it is the composer who organizes all the tones into a beautiful harmony. What the world needs now, he says, is a divine composer "to put us together on the staff of life, so we can combine to produce beauty, harmony, and peace." In music, this quality is developed through polyphony (many voices). A single instrument, like the violin, can capture the qualities of different species of human voice, such as soprano and mezzo-soprano. This polyphony is further differentiated by the different registers that exist within each species of voice. We do not know the extent of the Minister's knowledge of vocal registration, but in the above-mentioned comments (which clearly moved the members of the orchestra); he brings in a most valuable quality from outside formal musical study per se. The tendency in today's media-run culture is toward a homogenization, or flattening-out, of the differences both between unique individuals in Society, and between different voices and vocal registers in music. This habit undermines the idea that man is made in the image of God, because it flattens the quality that can only be manifested in the sovereign individual's creative mind.

A leader who works to develop creative individuals would tend to also orient toward such differentiation in music. Let's examine one example here. Mrs. Fohrman, in an early section of the video, mentions the talent Farrakhan demonstrates in playing the very difficult cadenza in the first movement. It must be noted that this cadenza is unique. Mendelssohn places it in the middle of the movement rather than the end, and it is clearly a tribute to the "Chaconne" for solo violin by J. S. Bach, a piece where Bach developed the principle of polyphony in a single instrument to undreamt-of heights. The Mendelssohn cadenza emphasizes a low voice, something most unusual. The violin most often plays in the soprano or mezzo-soprano range, but here we find the quality of a human tenor voice in its middle and lower registers! Farrakhan, though clearly capable of playing this passage with great speed, makes a point of slowing certain portions of it down, in order to make that very unique tenor voice sing, while playing the higher notes much more lightly. The videotape is highly recommended. We also think it would be a most valuable addition to the curriculum of any educational institution, from elementary school on up. And, we can only hope that Minister Farrakhan will continue to develop in this direction-something very sorely needed in music and in society today.

EIR Volume 22, Number 29, July 21, 1995

Farrakhan is Not the Problem: The Arrogance and Absurdity of America's Racial Litmus Test

By Tim Wise

Thirteen years ago, when I first started out on the lecture circuit, speaking about the issue of racism, it seemed as though everywhere I went, someone wanted to know my opinion of Louis Farrakhan.

To some extent, this was to be expected, I suppose. It was 1995, after all, and Farrakhan had just put together the Million Man March in DC. So when race came up, that, and sadly, the OJ Simpson trial and verdict seemed to be the two templates onto which white folks in particular would graft their racial anxieties.

Though OJ has long since faded as a matter of conversation among most, discussion of Farrakhan never seems to end. As controversy has erupted regarding comments made by Barack Obama's former pastor, the Rev. Jeremiah Wright, Wright's occasional words of praise for Farrakhan have caused many to suggest that he, and by extension, Obama, are somehow tainted. Wright, we are to believe, is forever compromised as a legitimate commentator on issues of race and even as a man of God. And why? In large part because he has noted two basic truths that are pretty hard to dispute: first, that Farrakhan is an important voice in black America–important in the sense that millions of black folks are interested in what he has to say–and second, that he is someone whose community work with young black men has been constructive where many other efforts to reach them have failed. Although Wright has never indicated that he agrees with the more extreme comments made by the Minister over the past two-and-a-half decades (and indeed, much of Wright's own ministry and approach to issues of race, gender and sexuality suggests profound disagreements with Farrakhan on these matters), his unwillingness to condemn the Nation of Islam leader is used to write him off as an extremist and a bigot.

As someone who is Jewish, I am expected to join in this chorus, apparently. Thus, the repeated and regular queries dating back at least fifteen years from other Jewish folks or from whites generally, asking why it is that I have never, in all of my years as an antiracist activist, turned my pen (or at least my computer keyboard) on Farrakhan.

But the simple truth is, Louis Farrakhan is not the problem when it comes to racism, sexism or heterosexism in this country; nor is he any real threat to Jews as Jews, or whites as whites, contrary to popular mythology.

Much as Muhammad Ali once famously noted that no member of the Vietcong had ever referred to him by a common racial slur, as a way to explain his lack of enthusiasm for fighting in Southeast Asia, I must point out that no member of the Nation of Islam ever told me when I was growing up that I was going to hell, that my soul was an empty vessel, or that I would burn in a lake of fire for all eternity, just like all of my Jewish ancestors, because we had rejected God. The folks who did that were white Christians: teachers, preachers, other kids, and co-workers–all of them spiritual terrorists and religious bigots of the first order. And not one of them was selling a bean pie on the corner, or copies of The Final Call. Yet, we as Jews make nice with Christians just like that, who smile while they condemn us, whose sense of spiritual superiority apparently causes us no alarm, nor spurs us to denounce them for their chauvinism, while the Nation of Islam's occasional episodes of anti-Jewish sentiment send us into fits of apoplexy.

But can we get real for a moment? What ability does Farrakhan have to do me any harm, or any Jew for that matter? When was the last time those of us who are Jewish had to worry about whether or not our Farrakhan-following employer was going to discriminate against us? Or whether our Fruit of Islam loan officer was going to turn us down for a mortgage? Or whether our Black Muslim landlord was going to screw us out of a rent deposit because of some anti-Jewish feelings, conjured up by reading the Nation's screed on Jewish involvement in the slave trade? The answer, of course, is never. If anything, members of the Nation, or black folks in general, have a much greater likelihood of being the victims of discrimination at our hands–the hands of a Jewish employer, banker or landlord, and certainly a white one, Jewish or not–than we'll ever have at theirs. White and/or Jewish bias against Nation members, either as blacks or Muslims or both, is more likely to restrict their opportunities than even the most advanced black bigotry is capable of doing to us. That's because bias alone is never sufficient to do much harm. Without some kind of institutional power to back up that bias, even the most unhinged black racism or anti-Jewish bigotry is pretty impotent.

Oh sure, a Black Muslim could attack me on the streets I suppose, either because of my whiteness or my Jewishness, so in that sense, the potential for such a person to harm me exists. But how many of us who are Jews have really been attacked by members of the Nation of Islam? Not only in absolute terms, but relative to the number who have been attacked or otherwise abused by white Christians? And why, given the likely answers to those questions, do we continue to fear the former, while spending so much time trying to ingratiate ourselves to the latter? Is their support for Israel–which is only offered because they hope ingathering Jews there will bring about the return of Jesus, at which point we'll all be sent to hell anyway–really that important? Is that all we require in order to be pimped?

Likewise, although lesbian, gay, bisexual and transgendered folks face violence regularly, and can be discriminated against legally in housing or employment, how often are members of the LGBT community singled out for these things by members of the Nation of Islam, as opposed to so-called God-fearing Christians filled with something to which these latter typically refer as "love?"

Sadly, it isn't only conservative and right-wing white folks who have chosen to make Farrakhan something of a racial Rorschach test for black leaders. To wit, the recent ventilations of self-proclaimed spiritual guru, Michael Lerner, who claimed in an April 29, 2008 e-blast from his "Network of Spiritual Progressives," that lasting damage had likely been done by Rev. Wright's praise for Farrakhan. According to Lerner, failure to clearly condemn the Nation of Islam leader is a "danger to any hopes of reconciliation between blacks and whites in this country."

But such a statement–in effect, placing the burden for racial reconciliation on black people, who must condemn Farrakhan in order for whites to be willing to dialogue–is a grotesque inversion of historic responsibility for the problem of racism in the United States.

Disturbingly, Lerner's formulation suggests it is perfectly legitimate for whites to hold blacks as a group responsible for the words of Louis Farrakhan, or the inadequate condemnation of Farrakhan by Rev. Wright. To believe that praise for Farrakhan is a deal-breaker when it comes to white-black amity, is to endorse the notion of collective blame: the same kind of thing Lerner rightly rejects when it is done to Jews. If someone were to suggest that Jewish folks' tepid condemnation of the Israeli government's repression of the Palestinians, or terrorist Jews like Meir Kahane–whose followers are welcomed participants each year in New York's "Israel Day Parade"–legitimizes anti-Semitism, or makes reconciliation between Jews and Muslims impossible, Lerner would be rightly outraged. But in his recent message, he engages in the same sloppy thinking.

Secondly, by arguing that praise for Farrakhan makes racial reconciliation impossible, Lerner essentially places the burden for solving the nation's race problem on blacks and blacks alone. Whites are not asked by Lerner to renounce popular white politicians or historical figures, even those with egregious records on issues of racial equity and justice. Only blacks must prove their sincerity by renouncing one of their own. It is as if Lerner believes Farrakhan were the reason for white folks' intransigence on issues of race; as if he honestly thinks whites had embraced the cause of racial equity until Farrakhan burst into the national consciousness sometime in the early 1980s. It's as if he thinks whites have been honest racial brokers, just waiting for blacks to come to the table of brotherhood, while blacks have been the impediment to progress because of their occasional kind words for the Minister. In other words, Lerner writes as if history never happened, or at least is of no consequence.

And speaking of history, for white Americans to condemn Farrakhan, while still admiring some of the people for whom we have affection–who have not only said but done far more evil things than he–is evidence of how compromised is the principle we now seek to impose on others. It is evidence of our duplicity on this subject, our utter venality as arbiters of moral indignation. It isn't that what Farrakhan has said about Jews, or gay and lesbian folks is acceptable–it isn't. But the fact that his words make him a pariah, while white folks actions don't do the same for us, is astounding.

After all, Louis Farrakhan never led a nation into war on false pretense. A white American president, supported in two consecutive elections by the majority of white people did that. And still, millions of whites are riding around with those infernal W stickers on the backs of their vehicles.

Louis Farrakhan never bombed a pharmaceutical factory in Sudan–responsible for making almost all of the drugs needed to fight major illness in that impoverished nation–on the false claim that it was a lab for chemical weapons. Another white American president, supported and revered by white liberals did that. And millions of white folks have been supporting that president's wife in her quest for the same office, at least in part to return to the glory days they felt were embodied by her husband's administration.

Louis Farrakhan never overthrew any foreign governments that had been elected by their people, only to replace them with dictators who were more to his liking. One after another white American president has done that, going back decades.

Louis Farrakhan didn't bomb the home of a foreign leader, killing his daughter in the process, or arm a rebel group in Nicaragua responsible for the deaths of over 30,000 civilians, or give guns to governments in El Salvador and Guatemala that regularly tortured and executed their people. One of white America's favorite white Presidents, Ronald Reagan did that. And millions of white folks (and pretty much only white folks) cried tears of nostalgia when he passed a few years ago, after which point thousands of these went to his ranch in California to pay tribute; and they name buildings and airports for him now; and some even suggest that his face should be added to Mt. Rushmore.

Louis Farrakhan didn't say that his adversaries should be hunted down until they no longer "remained on the face of the Earth." One of America's most revered white presidents, Thomas Jefferson, said that, in regard to American Indians. And he's on the two-dollar bill that I used to buy some coffee this morning.

And even if we were to restrict our comparative analysis to extreme statements alone, the fact is, white folks who say things every bit as bigoted as anything said by Farrakhan remain in good standing with the media and millions of whites who buy their books and make them best-selling authors.

Take Pat Buchanan, for instance. Despite a litany of offensive, racist and anti-Jewish remarks over the years, Buchanan remains a respected commentator on any number of mainstream news shows and networks, his books sell hundreds of thousands of copies, and rarely if ever has he been denounced by other pundits, or grilled by journalists, the way Farrakhan has been, in both cases.

So, for instance, Buchanan has said that AIDS is nature's retribution for homosexuality; that women are "not endowed by nature" with sufficient ambition or will to succeed in a competitive society like that of the United States; and that the U.S. should annex parts of Canada so as to increase the size of the nation's "white tribe" (because we were becoming insufficiently white at present), among other things.

Most relevant to demonstrating the hypocrisy of the press when it comes to Farrakhan, however, consider what Buchanan has said about Adolf Hitler. When Farrakhan said Hitler had been a "great" military and national leader-albeit a "wicked killer" (which is the part of the quote that normally gets ignored)-he was denounced as an apologist for genocide. Yet, when Buchanan wrote, in 1977, that Hitler had been "an individual of great courage, a soldier's soldier in the great war," a man of "extraordinary gifts," whose "genius" was due to his "intuitive sense of the mushiness, the character flaws, the weakness masquerading as morality that was in the hearts of the statesmen who stood in his path," it did nothing to harm his career, and has done nothing in the years since to prevent him from becoming a member of the pundit club in Washington. Nor would he receive the kind of criticism as Farrakhan-at least not lasting criticism-when he wrote in 1990 that survivors of the European Holocaust exaggerated their suffering due to "Holocaust survivor syndrome," and that the gas chambers alleged at Treblinka couldn't have actually killed anyone because they were too inefficient.

In other words, a white guy can praise Hitler, can cast aspersions on the veracity of Jews who were slotted to be killed, and can make blatantly racist, sexist and homophobic remarks and ultimately nothing happens to him, and no white politician is ever asked their opinion of him, or made to distance him or herself from the white man's rantings. But black folks will have to do the dance, will have to make sure to reject Farrakhan, because otherwise, apparently, we should intuit that they are closet members of the Nation, just waiting to take office so they can pop on a bow tie and put Elijah Muhammad's face on the nation's currency.

Perhaps when white folks begin to show as much concern for the bigoted statements and, more to the point, murderous actions of white political leaders as we show over the statements of Louis Farrakhan, then we'll deserve to be taken seriously in this thing we call a "national dialogue on race." Until then, however, folks of color will continue–and rightly, understandably so–to view us as trying to dodge our personal responsibility for our share of the problem. They will view us, and with good reason, as merely using Farrakhan so that we can divert attention from institutional discrimination, institutionalized white privilege and power, and the way in which white denial maintains a lid on social change, by creating the impression that everything is fine, and whatever isn't fine is the fault of crazy, militant black people, who follow crazy and hateful religious leaders.

In this way, white Americans can continue to pretend that the nation's racial problem isn't about us; that we are but passive observers of a drama concocted by others, over which only they have any control. And in this way, we guarantee the perpetuation of the very enmity we claim not to understand, the very tension we cannot comprehend, and the chasm-like divide that was created in our name and for our historic benefit, no matter how much we try and shift the blame now, heads rooted firmly in the proverbial sand.

Professor Derrick Bell's Analysis of Minister Farrakhan's "Racial Standing"

(Excerpted from Chapter 6: Rules of Racial Standing, Printed in Dr. Bells book)

Faces At The Bottom Of The Well)

Fourth Rule:

When a Black person or group makes a statement or takes an action that the white community or vocal components thereof deem "outrageous," the latter will actively recruit blacks willing to refute the statement or condemn the action. Blacks who respond to the call for condemnation will receive super standing status. Those blacks who refuse to be recruited will be interpreted as endorsing the statements and action and may suffer political or economic reprisals.

"Pretty strong stuff!" I exclaimed. "Meaning?" Geneva asked. "Well, perhaps the best contemporary example of the Fourth Rule involves the adverse reaction of many whites to the Muslim minister Louis Farrakhan. Smart and super articulate. Minister Farrakhan is perhaps the best living example of a black man ready, willing, and able to 'tell it like it is' regarding who is responsible for racism in this country. In this regard, he's easily a match for all those condescending white talk-show hosts who consider themselves very intelligent, certainly smarter than any black man.

"All these TV pros seem anxious to put this outspoken black man in his place. They have big staffs to do their research and prepare scripts filled to the brim with denigrating questions. And they have film clips carefully edited to make Farrakhan look as outrageous and irresponsible as possible.

"On camera, these self-appointed defenders of a society senseless enough to put them in their highly paid jobs, attack Farrakhan with a vengeance.

Clearly, destruction and not discussion is their aim. But there's no contest. Minister Farrakhan, calm, cool, and very much on top of the questions, handles these self-appointed guardians with ease. I love it!"

"I gather," Geneva broke in, "that many black people do not concur in your assessment of the Farrakhan phenomenon."

"It doesn't matter. Whatever their views on the controversial Black Muslim minister, every black person important enough to be interviewed is asked to condemn Minister Farrakhan — or any other truly outspoken black leader. Reporters generally ask, 'Have you heard what Farrakhan said and what are you going to do about it?' Note that, with Farrakhan, it's not what do you have to say, but what are you going to do about what he said? And don't make the mistake of telling a reporter ten positive things about Farrakhan and adding one criticism. You guessed it, the story will be headlined: 'Leading Black Spokesperson Condemns Farrakhan.'" "But," Geneva objected, "Farrakhan is a Black Muslim, which most blacks are definitely not."

"It's not his faith we're asked to deal with, Geneva. It's his race and his mouth."

She laughed. "On the surface, this is strange, kind of crazy. Remember the biblical story of how little David killed the mighty Goliath. David left his sheep in the field, journeyed to the impending battle, and convinced King Saul of the Israelites to allow him to be their champion. The armor they put on him was so heavy, he took it off, and went to meet Goliath with his staff, a slingshot, and five smooth stones in his pouch. And David was not modest or shy as he told Goliath what the Philistine giant least wanted to hear: This day will the Lord deliver thee into mine hand; and I will smite thee, and take thine head from thee; and I will give the carcasses of the host of the Philistines this day unto the fowls of the air, and to the wild beasts of the earth; that all the earth may know that there is a God in Israel. "For many people," Geneva continued, "Minister Farrakhan is a black David going one on one against the Philistines who bestride the land, abusing their power and generally messing over black folk. But when Farrakhan issues his challenge, no Goliath comes forth. Rather, some of the Philistines come running, not up to Farrakhan, but to any black person of substance they can find, asking, 'Did you hear what that man said about us? What are you going to do about it?' "

"That's the question I've been asking myself, Geneva," I responded. "Why must I do something about Minister Farrakhan? Those he condemns are not without power, not without money, not without guns. A sad history serves as proof that they know how to use all three against us. Why me?

"'Oh,' I am told, 'that man is hurting your cause.' But the cause of black people has been under attack for three hundred years, not by one black man but by the dominant white society. The suggestion that our current plight would be relieved if Farrakhan would just shut up is both naive and insults our intelligence. It also reveals more about those who would silence him than they likely want uncovered." I went on with how, in 1985, when Farrakhan was scheduled to speak in New York City's Madison Square Garden, Black officials came under heavy pressure to speak out and denounce him because of earlier statements of his deemed anti-Semitic and anti-white. Some black officials spoke out. Others, while not condoning some of Farrakhan's comments, complained in interviews that they were repeatedly expected to condemn fellow blacks for offensive remarks or behavior, while whites are not called upon to react to every such indiscretion by white officials. Typical of this position, Representative Charles B. Rangel (D., N.Y.) told a reporter that Farrakhan's statements about Judaism being a "dirty' religion" were "garbage," but added, "it's easy to come down heavy on Farrakhan." Rangel expressed the hope that matters had not reached the point that, just as blacks in South Africa have to carry a passbook to go from place to place, "black Americans have to carry their last statement refuting Farrakhan. I would not, if someone said Jesus Christ is a phony, go around asking Jews to sign a statement to condemn him."

In a similar vein, the Reverend Calvin O. Butts, pastor of the Abyssinian Baptist Church in Harlem, refused to condemn Farrakhan, and pointed out that the Muslim minister criticizes many groups in strong terms, including black churches and black ministers. Butts acknowledged that many Jewish people "look askance at any slight breeze of anti-Semitism. However," he added, "if in response to Israel's refusal to impose sanctions on South Africa to protest its policies of racial separation, I jumped up and said all Jewish leaders in the United States should denounce Israel, how many Jewish people would join me in that? I don't think many."

"I agree, Geneva," I said, "with both Congressman Rangeland the Reverend Butts. Anti-Semitism is a horrible thing, but just as all criticism of blacks is not racism, so not every negative comment about Jews — even if it is wrong — is anti-Semitism. Were I a Jew, I would be damned concerned about the latent — and often active — anti-Semitism in this country. But to leap with a vengeance on inflammatory comments by blacks is a misguided effort to vent justified fears on black targets of opportunity who are the society's least powerful influences and — I might add — the most likely to be made the scapegoats for deeply rooted anti-Semitism that they didn't create and that will not be cured by their destruction."

"Fear is not rational," Geneva observed. "Jews understandably feel that they must attack anti-Semitism whenever it appears. Farrakhan, being a frightening figure for most whites and thus vulnerable, becomes a symbol — even though, as you point out, an inappropriate one of the nation's anti-Semitism. Jews and white people generally hope that criticism by blacks will diminish his credibility, if not in the eyes of his followers, at least in the minds of those who believe that the threat he represents can be defused by our responding to their urgent pleas for black condemnation of an out-of-control black."

"It's not set out in the Fourth Rule, Geneva, but have you noticed that those blacks who utter 'beyond the pale' remarks are never forgiven. Thus, when Farrakhan attempts to explain that his statement was aimed at Israel as a state and not at Judaism as a religion, his explanation is rejected out of hand. The attitude seems to be: 'You said it, and thus you must be condemned for all time.' "

Geneva agreed. "The Reverend Jesse Jackson has experienced a similar 'lifetime renunciation' notwithstanding his frequent and fervent apologies for the regrettable 'Hymie and Hymietown' remarks he made during his 1984 presidential campaign. As I indicated earlier, I understand why a group is upset by what it deems racial or religious insults, but I doubt that I'm alone in not understanding why blacks who lack any real power in the society are not forgiven, while whites, including those at the highest levels of power, are pardoned. For example, many Jewish spokespeople complained bitterly when President Reagan went to lay a wreath at the Nazi cemetery at Bitburg in

Germany, but they do not continue to harass him about the issue everywhere he goes. No one denounced Reagan as anti-Semitic for going. More significantly, neither President Bush nor the whites who support him are called on to condemn Reagan in order to prove that they are not anti-Semitic.

"We boast that, unlike communist countries, there is no censorship of the press here. But blacks like Jesse Jackson, who are subject to an unofficial but no less effective 'renunciation,' are simply not heard."

"Your renunciation isn't limited to controversial political figures," I interrupted. "The writer bell hooks complains that 'often radical writers doing transgressive work are told not that it's too political or too "left," but simply that it will not sell or readers just will not be interested in that perspective.' "

"Similarly," she continued, "one need not agree with Farrakhan that African Americans need to separate from this country to understand that, after three hundred years of trying and not yet having the acceptance here that non-English-speaking white immigrants have on their first day on this soil, we need to be thinking of (if not yet doing) something other than singing one more chorus of 'We Shall Overcome.' Whatever his rhetorical transgressions. Minister Farrakhan and his church are giving the most disadvantaged black folk reason to hope when most of the country and more than a few of us blacks have written them off. His television hosts give him credit for cleaning up a neighborhood in Washington, D.C., and yet question his motives for accomplishing what few government officials have even seriously tried."

Thinking of Geneva's earlier statement about blacks who do not agree with our position on Farrakhan, I recalled a black friend who was unmoved when I discussed Farrakhan's abilities, and said, "Even if everything you say about him is correct, he is still a bigot. Why can't I call him what I think he is?" In effect, my friend was asking, "Even given the perverse weight white society gives to black-on-black criticism, must persons of color remain silent if they strongly disagree with statements or actions by other blacks?"

"The whole racial standing phenomenon, Geneva, raises a troublesome dilemma for many black scholars. How can blacks criticize other blacks or civil rights policies with which they disagree? Must they sacrifice their academic freedom, even their First Amendment right to free speech, in order to prevent whites from endowing with super standing their assertion of anti-black beliefs they have held all along?"

"The answer," Geneva said, "is that a burden of blackness, particularly for the black scholar, is racial awareness. Black academics must weigh the value of their statements, their writings, against the fact that, like it or not, their criticism of other blacks — whether or not accurate, or fair, or relevant — will gain them enhanced or super standing. In some instances, in 1991, the Nation of Islam and its Abundant Life Clinic received a citation from the City of Washington, D.C, for expunging Washington's Mayfair Mansions of violent crack dealing. The Nation of Islam continues to patrol the area."

They may feel so strongly about an issue or an individual that there is no alternative to speaking out — despite the predictable consequences." "I don't disagree," I responded, "but those who decide that, despite all, they must speak out against blacks who are threatening to whites, must not be surprised when blacks subjected to public criticism, cry 'Foul.' And when the black critics are later criticized themselves, this is not intended to — and certainly does not — silences the black speakers, as is claimed by Professor Stephen Carter. After all, they now have enhanced or super standing. White people want to hear their views, almost ad nauseam. Rather, some of the rest of us are saying, 'Now, see what you have done. Knowing the consequences, you should have communicated your criticism in some other way.' ""Is there an inconsistency," Geneva inquired, "in your opposition to blacks who gain enhanced standing by telling white people what they want to hear about blacks, and those like Minister Farrakhan who gain, if not standing, a kind of notoriety by telling whites what they least want to hear?"

"A good point," I conceded, "but I think the statements by Louis Farrakhan and other outspoken black militants are bold, impolitic, and sometimes outrageous precisely because they are intended for those blacks whose perilous condition places them beyond the courteous, the politic, even the civilities of racial and religious tolerance. These blacks need to hear their rage articulated by those able and willing to do so. They need reassurance that others, not they, are the cause of the wretched circumstances in which they live. Professor Lucius Barker makes this point when, while noting the large differences between whites and blacks regarding attitudes toward Farrakhan, he warns: 'Sooner or later whites must understand that this type of rhetoric and behavior has been fostered by their own ongoing maltreatment of blacks in the American political social order. As long as such conditions exist, blacks understandably find themselves more receptive to many types of rhetoric and promises of deliverance than would otherwise by the case.' "

"The real paradox here," said Geneva, "is that while whites fear spokespersons like Minister Farrakhan, the risk posed by the Farrakhans in this country is as nothing compared with the risks to all arising from the conditions against which those Farrakhan rails in uncompromising terms."

"I have not talked to him, Geneva, but I rather imagine that Minister Farrakhan understands the rules of racial standing. He knows that abstract condemnation of racism and poverty and the devastation of our communities is inadequate and ineffective. He has decided that the only way to be heard over the racial-standing barrier is to place the blame for racism where it belongs. Using direct, blunt, even abrasive language, he forthrightly charges with evil those who do evil under the racial structure that protects them and persecutes us, that uplifts them regardless of merit and downgrades us regardless of worth."

Farrakhan is Innocent, FBI is Guilty

Setting the record straight in Malcolm X Assassination

"Only one movement (The Black Muslims) though looked upon by disfavor by the major black civil rights groups, remains strong, consequential, cohesive, influential..."

-Phillip E. Hoffman, American Jewish Committee, 1972

"For years the Bureau has operated a counterintelligence program against the NOI and Muhammad...despite these efforts, he continues unchallenged in the leadership of the NOI and the organization itself, in terms of membership and finances, has been unaffected."

-Chicago Special Agent in Charge FBI Memo 4/22/1968

There is no doubt; the Unites States Federal Bureau of Investigation (FBI) has been a number 1 enemy of Black America. The crowning achievement of the FBI's COINTELPRO (counter-intelligence) program, during the 60's, were the assassinations of Rev. Dr. Martin Luther King Jr. and Malcolm X.

A new film called "Betty and Coretta" that is airing on the Lifetime network is working really hard to deceive the public. This oddly timed film features the wonderful R&B singer Mary J. Blige portraying the legendary Mrs. Betty Shabazz. The writers of this film include in its script accusatory words coming from Mrs. Shabazz, portrayed by Mary J. Blige, that Minister Farrakhan was responsible for her husband-Malcolm X's death.

The desire of the writers and producers are to destroy the magnetism of Minister Farrakhan among a new generation of Black youth that are discovering the living legend for the first time for themselves on college campuses and in the streets of the hood throughout America. This film is a weak attempt to derail Minister Farrakhan's momentum.

What do they want to derail, you might ask? Minister Farrakhan at nearly 80 years of age is more prolific than ever. He has recently toured the Caribbean nations addressing the governments, professional groups and youth groups. In 2012 Minister Farrakhan visited major historically Black college campuses and even delivered a major address at the University of California-Berkeley. During the heat of the summer, Minister Farrakhan mobilized the Nation of Islam's men's class, known as the Fruit of Islam, into the streets of Chicago and America's major cities on a peace in the streets mission. And in January of this year Minister Farrakhan began a 52 week webcast lecture series entitled The Time and What Must Be Done.

These are all activities that have historically been fought by the United States Federal Bureau of Investigation (FBI). J. Edgar Hoover used untold sums of tax payer dollars to wage a war against all Black Nationalist Groups. His stated goal was to prevent the rise of a Black "messiah" who could unite Black America in a bond of brotherhood and strength. Minister Farrakhan is the modern equivalent of what Hoover feared would happen 40 plus years ago.

This movie fits rightly in the category of what Hoover described in his COINTELPRO memos as "friendly media." Consider the following quoted from the famous Church Committee Report III. :

"Much of the Bureau's propaganda efforts involved giving information or articles to "friendly" media sources who could be relied upon not to reveal the Bureau's interests... the Division assembled a list of "friendly" news media sources -- those who wrote pro-Bureau stories. Field offices also had "confidential sources" (unpaid Bureau informants) in the media, and were able to ensure their cooperation. **The Bureau's use of the news media took two different forms: placing unfavorable articles and documentaries about targeted groups, and leaking derogatory information intended to discredit individuals.**"*(Church Committee Report III)*

In his very important book *Racial Matters: The FBI's Secret File on Black America 1960-1972*, Kenneth O'Reilly writes:

"In 1968 the Miami field office of the FBI and its "friendly and reliable" media contacts began work on a far more ambitious series of **documentaries** *on the Nation of Islam and other black groups."*

This film "Betty and Coretta" that disrespects and mocks the great legends of Black History is straight out of the FBI playbook. It is a "friendly media" documentary that aims to ruin the Nation of Islam. But this isn't the first time that the NOI has been under attack.

It is a well- known fact that the long term leader of the FBI, J. Edgar Hoover was a member of the Masonic Shrine. The Masonic Shriners are largely Christian white men who occupy powerful and influential positions within business, government and academic fields. They are students of the Bible, Holy Qur'an, World History and Prophecy. They are particularly known for their private veneration of Prophet Muhammad and the early history of Islam as a world conqueror.

Hoover's Shriner membership sheds light on his use of the word "messiah" in his infamous COINTELPRO memo. For in both Bible and Qur'anic prophecy, the Messiah is born from and is a blessing to the Children of Israel. The Messiah is to be a man like Moses. Moses liberated the enslaved Hebrews out of Egypt in the Biblical narrative. This led to the destruction of the Egyptian way of life and economy and produced the end of the rule of the wicked Pharaoh.

Ward Churchill and Jim Vander Wall write in their excellent expose *The COINTELPRO Papers* the following conclusion about the assassination of Malcolm X. This conclusion is informed by their meticulous research of the available documents on the nefarious government sabotage of Black movements.

By the point of Malcolm's assassination during a speech in Harlem on the night of February 14, 1965, the FBI had compiled at least 2,300 pages of material on the victim in just one of its files on him, the NOI and the OAAU." Malcolm X was supposedly murdered by former colleagues in the NOI as a result of the faction-fighting which had led to his splitting away from that movement and their "natural wrath at his establishment of a competing entity. However, as the accompanying January 22, 1969 memo from the SAC, Chicago, to the Director makes clear; **the NOI factionalism at issue didn't "just happen." Rather, it had "been developed" by deliberate Bureau actions - through infiltration and the "sparking of acrimonious debates within the organization," rumor-mongering, and other tactics designed to foster internal disputes – which were always the standard fare of COINTELPRO.** *The Chicago SAC, Marlin Johnson, who* *would shortly oversee the assassinations of Illinois Black Panther Party leaders Fred Hampton and Mark Clark, makes it quite obvious that he views the murder of Malcolm X as something of a model for "successful" counterintelligence operations.*

This may be a shocking conclusion, but it is the right conclusion. The FBI considered the assassination of Malcolm X a model for "successful" counterintelligence operations. And using Malcolm's assassination as a model, they proceeded to work to assassinate Fred Hampton and Mark Clark of the Black Panther Party!

They hope that they can assassinate Minister Louis Farrakhan. But Minister Farrakhan is a divinely guided man and a divinely protected man. He is completely innocent of Malcolm X's assassination. The FBI infiltrated and produced division within the Nation of Islam and worked diligently until their intended goal was achieved.

Black America must not allow itself to be deceived today, for this indeed is the day where the truth (the facts) shall make all free.

Farrakhan Vindicated!

Charges of anti-Semitism exposed as anti-Black racism, fear mongering and money scheme

In an interview with Democracy Now's Amy Goodman, the following exchange took place with former Israeli Education Minister Shulamit Aloni.

> *Amy Goodman: Yours is a voice of criticism we don't often hear in the United States. Often when there is dissent expressed in the United States against the policies of the Israeli government people here are called anti-Semitic. What is your response to that as an Israeli Jew?*
>
> *Shulamit Aloni: Well it's a trick, we always use it. When from Europe someone criticizes Israel we bring up the holocaust. When in this country people are criticizing Israel they are [called] anti-Semitic.*

What Ms. Aloni is describing is the very skullduggery used against the noble work and reputation of the Honorable Minister Louis Farrakhan and the Nation of Islam. Minister Farrakhan remains the beloved champion of truth and heroic strong man of the liberation struggle for poor and oppressed peoples around the world. Yet the price he has had to pay for speaking the truth is to suffer being called an anti-Semite and all that comes with that negative designation. However those who have falsely accused the Minister have actually revealed more about themselves and their true motives and intentions.

It is interesting that Ms. Aloni used the term "trick." According to Dictionary.com the word trick means:

> *A deception. Trick, artifice, ruse, stratagem, and wile are terms for crafty or cunning devices that are*

> *intended to deceive; an underhanded act designed to cheat someone; an artifice of diabolical ingenuity.*

The Most Honorable Elijah Muhammad taught that both the American slave master and the European colonizer of the Black, Brown, Red and Yellow peoples of the Earth did so using the science of "tricks and lies." Minister Aloni has confirmed the Most Honorable Elijah Muhammad's teaching in this regard by revealing one such trick that has been used against Minister Farrakhan and strong Black leaders throughout history. More plainly, the trick has been on the general public who are forced to admire, respect, support and even love Minister Farrakhan in veritable secret, or otherwise suffer by being accused of allowing their admiration to provide legitimacy for an alleged "anti-Semitic hate teacher." Some are affected by the trick to the point that they have developed outright negative opinions of Minister Farrakhan on the basis of his criticism of Jewish influence.

But to raise legitimate criticism to the level of anti-Semitism is fallacy known as the straw man fallacy. When legitimate criticism is mischaracterized as anti-Semitism, it is done obfuscate or hide real issues. The so-called anti anti-Semitic watchdog groups have even been condemned by avowed Farrakhan-critic Rabbi Michael Lerner. In his book, co-authored by Dr. Cornel West titled *Jews and Blacks: Let the healing begin* he writes.

> *The ADL, like the Simon Wiesenthal Center in Los Angeles, has built its financial appeal to Jews on its ability to portray the Jewish people as surrounded by enemies who are on the verge of launching threatening anti-Semitic campaigns. It has a professional stake in exaggerating the dangers, and sometimes allows existing racial or political prejudices in the Jewish world to influence how it will portray the potential dangers.*

And even though Rabbi Lerner is also guilty of "straw manning" Black criticism as Black Anti-Semitism, Rabbi Lerner understands the sources of Black criticism of the Jewish community. He wrote in 1969 that

> "Black anti-Semitism is ... a tremendous disgrace to Jews; for this is not an anti-Semitism rooted in ... hatred of the Christ-killers but rather one rooted in the concrete fact of oppression by Jews of blacks in the ghetto ... an earned anti-Semitism."

In the mistreatment of Minister Farrakhan by groups like the ADL and the Simon Wiesenthal Center, Black people *en masse* have been the real victim. For all of the economic programs and unity efforts advanced by Minister Farrakhan to uplift Blacks in America from poverty and want, have been undermined by these groups whose efforts are no less racist and anti-Black than that of the Ku Klux Klan. Maybe this is why when in 1991 Klan wizard David Duke ran for governor of Louisiana, the ADL was mute, claiming that their tax exempt status prevented them from intervening in a political campaign.

Yet, when in 1984 Rev. Jesse Jackson ran for the office of the President of the United States of America, the ADL actively engaged in sabotaging Rev. Jackson's campaign, even working to destroy his candidacy before it got started! According to Daniel Levitas of the Center for Democratic Renewal,

> "Before Jackson announced his candidacy in 1983, but aware of his impending run, the A.D.L. quietly circulated a nineteen-page memo to reporters detailing Jackson's past statements regarding Jews."

Matters got even worse when Rev. Jackson was accused by reporter Milton Coleman for using a Jewish racial slur when referring to Jews in New York. This caused Rev. Jackson to apologize publicly to the Jewish community for using the term "*Hymietown*," to which ADL director Nathan Perlmutter responded

> "He could light candles every Friday night, and grow side curls, and it still wouldn't mater...he's a whore."

No sane person would ever accuse Rev. Jesse Jackson as being a threat to the Jewish people. Still Perlmutter attacked Rev. Jackson whose run for the presidency symbolized the collective hopes and dreams of all Black people at that time. Perlmutter cared nothing for this fact; he viewed Blacks as a perennial "underdog," for whom no one would come to their aid once condemned by Jews. His vile reference to Rev. Jackson as a *whore* is definitely a tongue- in- cheek remark. By his own admission, the ADL practiced Black-baiting for money. In its own publication, *"Not the Work of a Day": ADL of B'nai B'rith Oral Memoirs, Vol. 1*, former ADL director Nathan Perlmutter reminisces:

> *A few weeks ago I had an expose [sic] on Jesse Jackson. Quite, by coincidence, I wasn't aware of it, we had one of those mass mailings going out for fund raising. It was one of those mailings to lists that were not our usual givers. The fund raising people tell me that in the several weeks following— these were small gifts, $20, $100, but there were many of them—we never had the response to a mailing that we had in our July, 1984 mailing.*

Author Micah L. Sifry in his 1993 article in *The Nation* magazine entitled *Anti-Semitism in America* seeks to hold these anti anti-Semitic groups accountable for their blatant hypocrisy in demonizing Blacks who are critical of their political and economic activities while at the same time, explaining away negative Jewish criticism made by whites.

Sifry points out that in 1990 political commentator Pat Buchanan blamed the Israel Lobby and Jewish geopolitical strategists for America's use of force against Saddam Hussein. Sifry notes that it was anti-Semitism watchdog Bill Buckley who defended Buchanan by writing that he did not believe that Buchanan was anti-Semitic but just *"attracted to mischievous generalizations."* Buchanan is interesting because he has enjoyed a popular and successful career in America as a Communications Director for Pres. Ronald Reagan and a frequent talk-show commentator. Yet he said that Adolf Hitler,

> was also an individual of great courage, a soldier's soldier in the Great War, a leader steeped in the history of Europe, who possessed oratorical powers that could awe even those who despised him. But Hitler's success was not based on his extraordinary gifts alone. His genius was an intuitive sense of the mushiness, the character flaws, the weakness masquerading as morality that was in the hearts of the statesmen who stood in his path." - *St. Louis Globe – Democrat, Aug 25, 1977*

Yet when Minister Farrakhan said that Hitler was "wickedly great,"(literally: one who is unusual or considerable in degree, power, intensity, in the practice of evil) the ADL and Wiesenthal Center used that harangue the Minister in the media and undermine his economic initiatives.

Sifry also notes Buchanan's orchestration of President Reagan's laying a wreath at the tomb of German SS soldiers. Sifry writes,

> *The Washington Post* reported that Buchanan was "credited... with the President's characterization of World War II German soldiers and SS troops as 'victims' of the Nazis 'just as surely as the victims in the concentration camps.' And that Buchanan bluntly urged Jewish leaders visiting the White House to 'be good Americans' and stop protesting Reagan's cemetery stop.""

According to Sifry, the ADL did not even raise any objection claiming that

> "There was an allegation about an offensive note about Jews [by Buchanan] at the time that we couldn't confirm."

But Reagan-Buchanan aside, they could be considered mild in comparison to the Fred Malek-Richard Nixon anti-Semitic combination. It is amazing to consider the response of the ADL to Fred Malek and President Nixon. According to Sifry,

> Fred Malek, a high level adviser to then-Vice President Bush had given President Nixon a list of Jews in the Labor Department, some of whom then lost their jobs.

To this the ADL's *Abraham Foxman called it*

> *"ancient history," adding that Malek had merely been "carrying out the instructions of an individual who had [prejudiced] feelings."*

We might understand Foxman's response as genuine were it not for what Sifry reveals of what the ADL wrote about the so-called individual who had [prejudiced] feelings that Malek worked for. The Watergate tapes of President Nixon reveal Nixon calling Jews kikes and lamenting their influence in the Arts and advising his staff to stay away from them. Yet according to Sifry,

> *he asked the A.D.L's research director, Alan Schwartz, for a copy of all statements the league had ever made regarding Nixon and anti-Semitism. The only one he could find was issued in response to the ex-President's assertion that lobbying by Israel and American Jews was responsible for Congressional opposition to the 1981 AWACS sale to Saudi Arabia. It read, in part: "Richard Nixon is indeed a friend of Israel and his views on foreign affairs merit regard. But singling American Jews out from the broad spectrum of opposition to the AWACS sale, is at best mischievous, at worst mean-spirited."*

In the light of this problematic history of the much feared charge of anti-Semitism, the fair minded observer is able to see clearly that what is motivating the use of this charge is not any real threat to the Jewish people and not any real anti-Semitic behavior. For when Jews in the Nixon administration lost jobs and income due to his anti-Jewish actions, he was still deemed a friend. When President Reagan and Pat Buchanan equaled the pain of German SS soldiers to those who were their victims, they are not even held accountable for such offensive behavior. So all we have left is the traditional tried and true blue racism that Black people have never had the luxury of being forgetting about. It is the same scapegoating of Blacks that has proven to be a money-maker whenever those in power can make those they influence to give them money in the name of protecting them from a Black boogeyman. Its time-out for these games and wasting of time and resources. If Minister Farrakhan is speaking falsehood, then all you have to do is respond to his call for a public showdown with him and defeat his falsehood with your truth.

Miracle Man of The Muslims

By Sterling X Hobbs

Sepia Magazine, May 1975

He's a better orator than the late Dr. Martin Luther King Jr. He sings better than Marvin Gaye. He's a better writer than Norman Mailer. He dresses better than Walt Frazier. He's more of a diplomat than Henry Kissinger. And he's prettier than Muhammad Ali.

Who can this be? Is it Superman? No, he's Minister Louis Farrakhan, the National Representative of the Nation of Islam, the Black Muslim followers of the Honorable Elijah Muhammad, and to his loyal "flock," he is all the aforesaid superlatives wrapped up in one magnificent species of manhood. Minister Farrakhan heads the powerful New York Muslim No.7 comprised of more than 5,000 active members and in his decade of its leadership has become a legend in his time, more than surpassing in dynamism and charisma all the claims for the late Malcolm X.

Louis Farrakhan is more sought after on college campuses than both Rev. Jesse Jackson and Dick Gregory. Many times he receives as much as $3,000 for his speeches, which he hands over to the Muslim school, the University of Islam. He addresses New York via radio six times per week and speaks regularly on the Muslim-funded national broadcast which reaches over 150 cities around the country. Regularly he receives ambassadors from foreign governments and has turned down invitations from both Idi Amin of Uganda and Fidel Castro of Cuba to visit their countries "with the full honors of a head of state." He has an open invitation to most Black-hosted television programs. He has been the subject of two TV specials. Last year Muslim Temple No. 7 published his first book, "Seven Speeches by Minister Louis Farrakhan" and later his first record – an album from his speech to over 70,000 Blacks on Randall's Island – was cut and entitled "Black Family Day 1974."

Observing Minister Farrakhan deliver a lecture is not unlike attending an exciting drama production or jamming at a rock concert. He transforms words into music and carries his listeners through thought-provoking ideology over the course which Blacks should take in economics, politics, religion and education. He acts out and illustrates his points and the screams from women are reminiscent of the old Temptations concerts.

Many observers of the racial scene, who had written off the Nation of Islam after the death of Malcolm X and the end of Black militancy in the late 60s, now ask: "Where did this man come from?" Black Muslims will smile and say: "One morning as the sun rose in the east, New Yorkers awoke from slumber and found that suddenly the Black Muslims, like Jesus, were resurrected from the dead and were led by a minister more fiery and articulate than ever. And the Muslims became once again a power to reckon with."

My first experience with Minister Farrakhan came five years ago at the Congress of African Peoples in Atlanta. I was seated with Black poet Don L. Lee among the dashikis and African agbadas, wearing my own of course. Suddenly following an address by the late Urban League leader, Whitney Young, a host of Black Muslim brothers walked swiftly into the arena and replaced the security guards who had been provided by Imamu Amiri Baraka, coordinator of the conference.

Each of the Muslim brothers appeared to be at least 6 foot 3 and consequently Minister Farrakhan, who stands about 5 foot 9, was dwarfed in their company. My first reaction was, "Wow, you mean this little dude is Louis Farrakhan?" I had heard so much about him that I was expecting a giant, one who would be in physical harmony with the legends.

Then Minister Farrakhan began to speak. His voice thundered throughout the auditorium and each time the audience would erupt in applause, he would say, "Shut up and listen! You clap too much and think too little." And the audience loved each minute of it. In a manner which is completely his own, he denounced the entire Baraka-inspired Pan-African movement. He called their leaders unfit and challenged them to "ask yourself the question: Am I qualified to lead Black people?" Come on up with the answer. And don't lie to yourself; you've been lying long enough!" The arena went wild, the audience loving it. Then he denounced them for their "immorality" and they begged for more. Needless to say I was awed.

I recall my first visit to his office back in 1972. I was doing an article for a community newspaper and I was as nervous as a schoolgirl in the exclusive company of Ringo Starr. But Farrakhan's manner was pleasant and comforting. He had just finished making a two-hour speech and was preparing to do yet another. Perspiration soaked his entire body as he asked, "Do you mind if I change clothes while we talk?" The minister stripped down to his shorts as I asked questions. Lester 4X, his assistant secretary came in with a fresh shirt from the Libas clothing store. The sleeves were a bit too long and Farrakhan, in mock anger, said, "Man you brought me this jive-time shirt. I ought to..." then threw his hands up as if he were about to mix it up with his secretary. "The Messenger told me to never go before the people without fresh clothes, else you'll get sick," he said. I have accompanied Farrakhan on some of his visits to college campuses and to watch him before student audiences is fascinating. He never uses notes but prefers to fire away freely. "I was born to do this work," he once said. "This is a labor of love. I love Black people and that's why I don't have to use notes. Have you ever seen a man in love refer to his notes when he's talking to the one he loves? Well, I'm in love with my Black brothers and sisters and I don't need notes because what I say is from my heart, not a notebook."

Often the Minister doesn't even select his subject matter until after he is before is audience and making his opening remarks. He is astonishingly sensitive to people's thinking and ideological leaning. At Cheney State College, for example, he was quite fiery and related much of his message in "street talk" because this is the type of campus Cheney is. Then later that same day, at Lincoln University, he was on a higher spiritual plane because Lincoln has a strong religious element on campus knowledgeable in scriptures. But the uncanny thing is that no one has to tell him this, but he feels it when he goes out and faces his audiences.

In the wake of the passing of Elijah Muhammad, there was much talk of a power struggle in the Nation of Islam and that Minister Louis Farrakhan was a prime candidate to succeed the Messenger of Allah. But he was among the first to pledge fealty to Wallace Muhammad and let all know that he has no aspirations whatsoever for Muhammad's exalted position among Muslims. In his book, "The Black Muslims in America," C. Eric Lincoln quotes him: "The Messenger has very big shoes and my feet are too small." But the distrust of him in some circles troubled Farrakhan to the point that he went to Chicago to inform Muhammad prior to his death: "Dear Apostle, I fear turning a hypocrite to the truth." And Muhammad replied, "Brother, you don't have that to worry about – not you."

Minister Farrakhan reinforces his position with statements like: "Elijah Muhammad is my master. When he found me I was just a dumb Negro slave, a dope user, a wine drinker and a disrespecter of the Black woman. He is the greatest, most wise man the Earth has ever produced."

He constantly reminds his audience that "without Muhammad I am nothing." He once said: "Elijah Muhammad gave Malcolm wings and after flying for so long and so high, Malcolm began to think that he was flying under his own power. I know who has given me my wings and I know who controls those wings even now. I'm sitting in the driver's seat here in New York, but Elijah Muhammad is doing the steering."

There are many Muslims who believe Farrakhan to be the modern-day equivalent of Moses' brother Aaron in the Bible and Holy Qur'an. The words and legacy of the Muhammad, they feel, will lead Black people forma 400-year bondage in America as Moses led the children of Israel from bondage in Egypt under Pharaoh. Some see a parallel between scriptural Aaron, the chief spokesman for Moses, and Minister Farrakhan.

When he was scheduled to appear on Black Journal with Elijah Muhammad on a panel featuring Imamu Amiri Baraka, Rev. Albert Cleage, Rev. Ralph Abernathy and Vernon Jordan, Minister Farrakhan shouted: "This will be Moses and Aaron conquering Pharaoh's magicians."

Beyond his oratorical skill, Minister Farrakhan has demonstrated that he is also an accomplished business administrator, personally directing the opening of nearly a score of flourishing Muslim businesses in New York. Sales figures of the New York Temple alone were well over $3 million last year.

The most visible Muslim sections in New York are around 116th St. and Lenox Avenue in Harlem where the Arabian-designed Temple No.7 is located. On the two streets, there are 15 Muslim-owned establishments.

Muslim enterprises employ more than 500 people, not all of whom are Muslim. There are more than 50 businesses privately owned and operated by individual Muslims with portions of their profits donated to the Muslim cause.

Sales grosses of Muslim business units range from up to $15,000 weekly for Muslim Brand Imported Fish (the profit margin in fish is quite high, states Minister Larry 4X) to $7,000 weekly for the bean pie distribution of Shabazz Bakery in Corona. Minister Larry once said, "Without the bean pie we'd have to close down," before Farrakhan took over administration of New York Muslim businesses.

Real estate holding alone of the Muslims in New York are about $1,730,000.

To administer the New York temple and its business ventures, Farrakhan arrives at his office within the Islamic Complex at 7:30 a.m. He usually is driven in his Mercedes 600 or on days when he feels daring, he drives himself to work in either his Eldorado or Mercedes sports car. He's normally greeted by five or six brothers who act as a security force which he does not necessarily desire. Out of respect a brother will usually open Farrakhan's door or attempt to carry his briefcase and Farrakhan will plead, "Please, brother, I'm not an invalid…allow me to carry my own bag."

Minister Farrakhan was born Louis Gene Walcott in the Bronx in New York City of Jamaican parents who later moved to Boston's Roxbury section. His mother sought to give him a musical background and he became regarded as a boy-genius at playing the violin. In school he was particularly interested in English and he searched for a more complete knowledge of the Black man's history. He was a star athlete at English High, winning track honors in the 100-yard dash.

When he was a child, his mother taught him about the lynching of Blacks in the South and she would give him books on slavery. So moved was young Louis over Black suffering of slaves that tears would stream down his cheeks. Later Louis attended Winston-Salem Teachers College in North Carolina, and experienced the Dixie discrimination that he had read about.

Of his childhood, Minister Farrakhan remembers: "Once my showed me a picture on his wall of a man whom he said was the greatest leader our people had ever had. I stood on a chair and looked into this man's face for many long minutes. Then I asked my uncle, 'Where is this man, that I might meet him and help him?' My uncle answered, 'That man is dead.' I was so hurt that after hoping, all my young years, to meet the right man for our people, that when I found him, he was already dead. Tears rolled down my cheeks and I cried and cried because Marcus Garvey was dead."

Louis Walcott became a professional singer and actor, struggling to make it big with calypso and country songs. He still plays whenever the mood hits him or when he requires a break from the constant pressure he's under. Diners at the Salaam No. 7 Restaurant were shocked one Saturday evening to find the live entertainment supplied by Minister Farrakhan himself who, with a quartet of Muslim brothers, played the violin and sang a number of songs.

While working in a Boston night club when he was 20, a Muslim brother came up to him and announced, "Brother, God has chosen a Messenger to lead the Black man to freedom, justice and equality." Quite emotional, Louis Walcott left the night club, walked slowly down Massachusetts Avenue, crying and talking to God: "Oh God, You know I have always loved my people. Why did not you choose me?" Later he had the thought: "When God chose His Messenger I was not even born. And if God had chosen a Messenger, that choice is all right with me. Let me find the Messenger then and serve him as I would serve God."

While in Chicago in 1955 at a Muslim Saviours' Day Convention, he heard Elijah Muhammad speak for the first time and thought to himself that he didn't particularly like the Messenger's style of speech. Then something very eerie took place. Out of the thousands of people in attendance, Mr. Muhammad looked up into the row of seats where Louis was sitting and said, "Brother, don't pay attention to how I speak, pay attention to what I'm saying Brother. I didn't get the chance to go to the white man's fine schools because when I tried to go, the doors were closed. But if you take what I say and place it into the beautiful way of speaking you know, you can help me save our people."

Louis was stunned. "Man, that scared me to death," Farrakhan relates. "I thought the Messenger had read my mind." But what Louis didn't know was that Muslim captain had told Mr. Muhammad where Louis would be seated and informed the Messenger that Louis "was a college man who could help us if we get him." But how the Messenger knew what Louis was thinking remains a mystery.

Following this experience, Gene Walcott registered with the Nation of Islam's New York Temple. Louis X soon rose to become a lieutenant in the Fruit of Islam, the name given to the military training of men who belong to Islam. Every male Muslim is considered an F.O.I. after he undergoes his processing period.

Though the martial arts are taught, the greater portion of the F.O.I. classes are spent discussing proper marital relationships, proper grooming, techniques in salesmanship, and spiritual meanings of the Bible and Holy Qur'an.

The only cases where the F.O.I. is used for physical punishment is in rare cases of the abuse of a fellow Muslim, especially a Muslim sister. In this case the offender, if found guilty, is penalized according to his offenses. Once a Muslim sister's pocket book was snatched and the thief was apprehended. The beating he received left few unbroken bones in his body. I am told that an offense such as rape of a sister could possibly result in the death of the offender.

But the F.O.I. classes stress a peaceful relationship with the community at large. However, the Muslim realize that a degree of respect must be maintained and they fear if they allow transgressors to go unpunished then "Laz" – the nickname from the Biblical Lazarus used to describe non-Muslims – would declare open seasons on Muslims. But Farrakhan reminds some overzealous members of his congregation that "Allah gives you no credit for beating up your mentally-dead Black brother."

When he was known as Louis X, Farrakhan rapidly grew in stature, received a promotion and was transferred to the Boston Temple to become F.O.I. Captain. When something happened to the temple minister, "I received word that I was to minister to the people," Minister Farrakhan recalls.

Ministering, at first, did not come easily to a young and inexperienced Louis X. "I was not able to relate to many of the educated persons who joined the Boston Temple as they were much more intelligent than I. And because I couldn't understand their ideas, I thought they were enemies of Islam and I drove them all out of the temple," he relates.

Realizing his mistake, Louis X wrote to the Messenger in Chicago and asked to be relieved of his position and charged with "any sins they commit wile expelled from the Temple." This display of compassion pleased the Messenger and instead of dismissing Minister Louis, he permitted the suspended brothers to return to the Temple and Louis X remained the minister. Coupled with his administrative problems, Louis X had financial difficulties to add to his woes, "I was so poor in Boston that once, when I spoke in Philadelphia, and the holes in my shoes were so large that the brothers had to drive me right up to the door of the Temple to keep the rain from soaking."

Finally, around 1960, Minister Louis, having more experience and maturity, saw his problems begin to ease. During that period Louis X recorded a song, "A White Man's Heaven Is A Black Man's Hell." He also authored two plays: "Orgena" (A Negro spelled backwards) and "The Trial." Among Muslims these were quite popular and Louis X was beginning to make a name for himself traveling throughout the country performing his two plays for community audiences.

But one evening the Honorable Elijah Muhammad asked him, "Brother do you want to be a song and dance man or a do you want to be my minister?" There was no question in his mind about his reply: "I want to be your minister, Dear Holy Apostle."

Minister Louis was moved to New York after the defection of Malcolm X, a somewhat ironic move because prior to this they had been close friends. Malcolm admitted Louis was closer to him than his own blood brothers. But Malcolm's crusade the last year of his life to undermine the work of the Nation destroyed this closeness and Minister Louis openly attacked Malcolm in Muhammad's Speaks as a hypocrite and "deadly enemy of the Black man."

Soon after this move to New York, Elijah Muhammad gave him the name "Farrakhan." The Messenger never revealed the exact meaning of Minister Farrakhan's name and to this day he is unaware of what his name means.

Minister Farrakhan is a personable man who generally likes people and enjoys sharing ideas with most anyone. This has enabled him to establish warm relationships with most community leaders in New York. Though he chooses to shy away from the word "diplomat," Farrakhan is just that. But his style of diplomacy is rarely based upon shrewd deception, but rather upon honest appreciation for opinions of others. And while he may disagree with their ideologies, his love for them as brothers is felt in his voice and seen in his eyes during meetings with them. He says, "We can disagree without being disagreeable."

Minister Farrakhan's power internally is growing daily. Thousands of young Blacks have joined the Black Muslims after hearing one of Farrakhan's fiery lectures delivered in person or over radio or television. And while he was only 22 when he became a Minister, he is now revered as a "big brother" to many of the younger Black Muslims."

Is Farrakhan the New Garvey?

The new Lifetime Network film entitled Betty and Coretta is extremely offensive to Black America. How in the world could a film be rolled out during Black History Month that offers such ugly caricatures of our powerful Black heroes and there not be national outrage. How could the Sanitsky company be allowed to premier this wickedly motivated film during this very special Black History Month? Black History Month is very significant because it comes in the aftermath of the inauguration of America's first Black President's second term. And while Blacks bask in the tremendous accomplishment of President Obama, a blow to the legends of our history comes out of nowhere to sucker-punch the Black electorate when they least expected it.

As a student of the Honorable Minister Louis Farrakhan, I am intrigued by the fact that this film has all the hallmarks of the documentaries and films that were produced in the 50's and 60's at the height of the infamous COINTELPRO program of the FBI. These films were designed to destroy the magnetism and popularity of the strong Black American dissidents who were seeking to hold America accountable for centuries of mistreatment, injustice and inequality. And while this film mocks a broad group of our leaders, Minister Louis Farrakhan is depicted in the worst light. This movie places the blame for the murder of Malcolm X onto Minister Louis Farrakhan.

This horrible lie against the Minister should concern all in the Black community. Because despite there being a Black man in the White House as President of the United States, he is burdened with trying to be everything to everybody. Therefore his benefit to the Black community is diluted and virtually ineffectual. Minister Farrakhan on the other hand, has no such burden and is free to be a gallant strong man and hero for Black causes. Minister Farrakhan has demonstrated a great deal of love, humility and an impressive ability to forgive other Black leaders who repudiate and speak ill of him to appease white and Jewish concerns. He has always been generous in lending his credibility with the masses to defend Blacks in trouble. He openly defended Marion Barry, Rep. Alcee Hastings, David Dinkins, Rev. Jesse Jackson, Michael Jackson and numerous others. This is a function and outgrowth of his profound love for his people and what God has given him of a special wisdom that allows him to see the hidden hand of Satanic forces at work in the undoing of the Black community.

The Minister is at the root of the most powerful event in modern history. The Million Man March in 1995 brought out between 1.6 and 1.8 million Black Men of all faiths, ages and walks of life for the noble purpose of atonement, reconciliation and responsibility. That event, more than any other event, clearly communicated Minister Farrakhan's value and importance to more than just the Nation of Islam. We learned at the Million Man March that Minister Farrakhan had become the most influential man in all of America.

Minister Farrakhan's ability to attract and impact the lives of millions of people with the message of self-love, Black nationhood, and divine destiny is reminiscent of one of the great patriarchs of Black people's struggle for liberation, the Honorable Marcus Mosiah Garvey.

Marcus Garvey's United Negro Improvement Association attracted between 6 and 8 million followers. Both Marcus Garvey and Minister Farrakhan's wide appeal made them targets for the FBI's anti-messiah objectives. COINTELPRO memos outlined the specific denial objective *"to prevent the rise of a "messiah" who could unify, and electrify, the militant Black Nationalist movement."* That Hoover feared Black nationalists being "unified" and "electrified," reveals what Hoover understood of Biblical prophecy. The Bible in Ezekiel 37:10 speaks of a people referred to as "dry bones". These despondent and life-less people are the subject of the Prophet Ezekiel's ministry. Ezekiel, who is considered a type of the Messiah, causes these "dry bones" to come alive and to become "unified" into what the Bible calls and "exceedingly great army." Hoover therefore understood Black people's place within Biblical prophecy.

The behavior of the FBI towards both Garvey and Minister Farrakhan indicate that both have been viewed as the political and prophetic messiah. Minister Farrakhan might be considered the New Garvey or New Messiah as both he and Garvey bear striking similarities to one another as revealed in a 1919 Department of Justice memo written by J. Edgar Hoover.

In Race First by Professor Tony Martin a memo is included that is dated October 11, 1919 from the Department of Justice that describes just why the Honorable Marcus Mosiah Garvey was considered dangerous. In the memo Hoover is disappointed that *"Unfortunately, he (Garvey) has not as yet violated any federal law whereby he could be proceeded against on the grounds of being an undesirable alien, from the point of view of deportation. It occurs to me, however, from the attached clipping that there might be some proceeding against him for fraud in connection with his Black Star Line propaganda..."*

The Memo continues with Hoover's description of Garvey and his work:

> DEPARTMENT OF JUSTICE,
> WASHINGTON, D C
>
> J.E.H-FBO
>
> October 11, 1919.
>
> MEMORANDUM FOR MR. RIDGELY.
>
> I am transmitting herewith a communication which has come to my attention from the Panama Canal, Washington office, relative to the activities of MARCUS GARVEY. Garvey is a West-Indian negro and in addition to his activities in endeavoring to establish the Black Star Line Steamship Corporation he has also been particularly active among the radical elements in New York City in agitating the negro movement. Unfortunately, however, he has not as yet violated any federal law whereby he could be proceeded against on the grounds of being an undesirable alien, from the point of view of deportation. It occurs to me, however, from the attached clipping that there might be some proceeding against him for fraud in connection with his Black Star Line propaganda and for this reason I am transmitting the communication to you for your appropriate attention.
>
> The following is a brief statement of Marcus Garvey and his activities:
> Subject a native of the West Indies and one of the most prominent negro agitators in New York;
> He is a founder of the Universal Negro Improvement Association and African Communities League;
> He is the promulgator of the Black Star Line and is the managing editor of the Negro World;
> He is an exceptionaly fine orator, creating much excitement among the negroes through his steamship proposition;
> In his paper the "Negro World" the Soviet Russian Rule is upheld and there is open advocation of Bolshevism.
>
> Respectfully,
>
> J. E. Hoover

1. **Garvey is a native of the West Indies and one of the most prominent Negro agitators in New York.** (Minister Farrakhan's parents are both from the West Indies. Minister Farrakhan as the Honorable Elijah Muhammad's minister in New York City from 1965-1975 was considered the most powerful Black leader in New York during that time. It bears noting that Hoover's use of "agitator" is in a negative or pejorative sense. But the

agitator has a very positive connotation when it describes the large cylindrical moving part inside a clothes washing machine. It is the dirt and grime on the clothes that is agitated and removed from the clothing in an effort to make the clothes clean and wearable. Black leadership therefore should take pride in being called an agitator to cleanse America of its disease of racism, injustice and inequality that keeps a stain on any global mention of the United States.)

2. He (Garvey) is a founder of the Universal Negro Improvement Association and African Communities League. (Minister Farrakhan in his leadership role within the Nation of Islam has articulated and espoused similar if not identical political and social positions as that of Marcus Garvey's UNIA. The Minister also served as deputy commander of the World Islamic People's Command. His leadership also produced the National African American Leadership Summit-NAALS and the Millions More Movement)

3. He (Garvey) is promulgator of the Black Star Line and is the managing editor of the Negro World. (Minister Farrakhan is the promoter of several cooperative economic initiatives in the same vein of Garvey's Black Star Line, for example the Power Personal Care Products Line, NOI Security, and the 3 Year Economic Savings Program. Garvey was the managing editor of the Negro World newspaper; Minister Farrakhan is the publisher of the Final Call Newspaper. Both leaders understand the power of the printed word and the distribution of positive messages in the transformation of their communities.)

4. He (Garvey) is an exceptionally fine orator, creating much excitement among the Negroes through his steamship proposition. (Minister Farrakhan is without a doubt, the most exceptional orator ever produced for the articulation and advocacy of Black causes. The Minister's speeches, programs and initiatives routinely produce excitement among all who listen. In 1994 Time magazine documented that Minister Farrakhan had a 67% approval rating in the Black community. It was the Minister's mighty voice that produced the great Million Man March. Statistics revealed that 80% of the men who attended were of the Christian faith. So the power of the Minister's delivery of the divine revolutionary message is evidenced in this statistic which shows how what he speaks is not contained within the narrow confines of any one particular religion or ideology. His voice is the universal sound that the oppressed hear and respond to as though it is the voice of God.)

Minister Farrakhan like Marcus Garvey has broken no laws. This is upsetting to his enemies who want a reason to arrest him and destroy his movement. Like Garvey he has the attention and support of millions. The Black community at-large should rally around the Minister and demand that the governments classified files on the Nation of Islam and all Black groups be released and un-redacted. Black people have suffered too much to continue on believing that our movements and our leaders are failures, turn-coats and murderers of one another. We deserved the once hidden hand of government to be revealed so that justice and healing can come as the product of our full access to truth.

Bibliography

Ajanaku, Karanja. 2009. "Minister Louis Farrakhan: 'I Am Exactly What I Am'." *The New Tri State Defender.* October 22. Accessed August 13, 2013. http://www.tsdmemphis.com/index.php/news/4779-.

Alexander, Amy. 1998. *The Farrakhan Factor.* New York: Grove Press.

Allen, Frederick. 1985. "Farrakhan's Real Message Has Validity." *Executive Intelligence Review*, December 13: 71.

Associated Press. 1998. "Bruce Willis Calls Farrakhan a Hero." *AP News Archive Beta.* June 15. Accessed August 9, 2013. http://www.apnewsarchive.com/1998/Bruce-Willis-Calls-Farrakhan-a-Hero/id-5fbcba2e9223183a05a881b157305f11.

Badu, Erykah. 2013. "@fatbellybella." *Twitter.com.* April 17. Accessed August 10, 2013. https://twitter.com/fatbellybella.

Beiser, Vince. 1997. "Farrakhan Talks To The Jews." *Jewish World*, June 26: 26.

Bell, Derrick. 1993. *Faces At The Bottom Of The Well: The Permanence of Racism.* New York: Basic Books.

2003. *Journey in Black: Minister Louis Farrakhan.* Directed by John Bellamy. Performed by Black Entertainment Television.

Blige, Mary J. 2013. "@MaryJBlige." *Twitter.com.* February 12. Accessed August 10, 2013. https://twitter.com/maryjblige.

Cheney, Charise L. 2005. *Brothers Gonna Work it Out: Sexual Politics in the Golden Age of Rap Nationalism.* New York: NYU Press.

Comer, Matt. 2012. "Councilwoman LaWana Mayfield addresses Farrakhan controversy ." *The Clog.* November 14. Accessed August 10, 2013. http://clclt.com/theclog/archives/2012/11/14/councilwoman-lawana-mayfield-addresses-farrakhan-controversy.

Executive Intelligence Review. 1985. "Young Mostly Agrees With Farrakhan." *Executive Intelligence Review*, September 13: 63.

1997. *Gray's Ferry Unity Peace Rally.* Directed by The Final Call Inc. Performed by Hon. Min. Louis Farrakhan.

1997. *International Islamic Conference.* Directed by Final Call Publishing. Performed by Honorable Minister Louis Farrakhan.

Farrakhan, Minister Louis. 1993. *A Torchlight For America.* Chicago: Final Call Publishing.

FCNN. 2011. "Minister Farrakhan, Wyclef Jean on Haiti TV & Radio ." *YouTube.* December 16. Accessed August 10, 2013. http://www.youtube.com/watch?v=v0Au2J83800&list=PL2A7710178CE5A09F.

Fields, Gary, and Maria Puente. 1996. "The Million Man March: A Movement Or Just A Moment." *USA Today*, October 10.

Franklin, Robert Michael. 2001. "Religious Belief and Political Activism in Black America: An Essay." *Journal of Religious Thought* 63-72.

Freeman, Debra Hanania. 1993. "Farrakhan Dispels Media Image." *Executive Intelligence Review*, May 21: 63.

Gardell, Mattias. 1996. *In The Name of Elijah Muhammad: Louis Farrakhan and The Nation of Islam.* Durham, NC: Duke University Press.

Gates, Hernry L. 1995. "Grading Farrakhan." *The New Yorker Magazine*, October 30: 8.

Giovanni, Nikki. 1996. "A Million Reasons To Hope." *Black Collegian* 3: 26-28.

G-Unit Radio 19. 2013. "50 Cent - Louis Farrakhan Skit ." *YouTube.com.* March 29. Accessed August 10, 2013. http://www.youtube.com/watch?v=_6Ob8v67dE8.

Henry III, William, Sylvester Monrie, Sharon Epperson, Julie Johnson, and Ann Blackman. 1994. "Ministry of Rage." *Time Magazine*, February 28: 21-27.

Hilburn, Robert. 1988. "POP MUSIC : Public Enemy's Chuck D: Puttin' on the Rap." *Los Angeles Times.* February 7. Accessed August 9, 2013. http://articles.latimes.com/1988-02-07/entertainment/ca-41167_1_public-enemy.

Hobbs, Sterling X. 1975. "Miracle Man of The Muslims." *Sepia Magazine*, May: 24-31.

Hume, Ellen. 1984. "Storm Center: Racial Rhetoric Puts Farrakhan in Spotlight In Jesse Jackson Camp --- Black Muslim's Controversy Seems To Help Campaing, Origins of the Friendship; Influence of The Golden Rule." *Wall Street Journal*, April 26: 1.

Jestice, Phyllis G. 2004. *Holy People of The World: A Cross Cultural Encyclopedia.* Santa Barbara, CA: ABC-CLIO,Inc.

Jones, Frank Paul. 1996. "Is Farrakhan The Solution To Our Problem ." *New Amsterdam News*, October 18.

Jones, William. 1993. "Black Caucus, NOI Agree To Closer Collaboration." *Executive Intelligence Review*, October 1: 68.

Jordan, Robert A. 1983. "Jackson speech was not best at Washington Rally." *Boston Globe*, September 1: 1.

Kane, Gregory. 1996. "What I'm about to say will no doubt get me in trouble with the Jewish community. Protesters w." *The Baltimore Sun.com.* September 22. Accessed August 10, 2013. http://articles.baltimoresun.com/1996-09-22/news/1996266058_1_louis-farrakhan-kemp-nation-of-islam.

Karenga, Maulana, and Haki R. Madhubuti. 1996. *Million Man March/Day of Absence: A Commemorative Anthology.* Chicago: Third World Press.

Larry King/CNN. 2013. "Mike Tyson Expresses His Love Of Farrakhan." *YouTube.* June 20. Accessed August 10, 2013. http://www.youtube.com/watch?v=i4ge5mOH0wo.

Lester, Julius. 1985. "The Time Has Come." *New Republic*, October 28: 11-12.

Lion, Snoop. 2013. "Snoop Dogg AKA Snoop Lion speaks of what The Hon. Louis Farrakhan has meant to his life ." *YouTube.* June 27. Accessed August 10, 2013. http://www.youtube.com/watch?v=h3S5FPAglO8.

MacNeil Lehr News Hour. 2012. "Bell: Farrakhan 'Great Hero For The People'." *Breitbart.com.* March 9. Accessed August 10, 2013. http://www.breitbart.com/Breitbart-TV/2012/03/09/Bell%20Louis%20Farrakhan%20is%20A%20Great%20Hero%20For%20The%20People.

Marsh, Clifton E. 2000. *The Lost Found Nation of Islam in America.* Eugene,OR: Wipf and Stock.

McCall, Nathan. 1995. "Makes Me Wanna March; Why I'm Coming and What All of Us Have To Gain." *The Washington Post*, October 15: C01.

Media Matters for America. 2008. "Ignoring Obama's statement on Trumpet award, Hannity suggested that Obama "associated" himself with Farrakhan ." *Media Matters for America.* January 18. Accessed August 9, 2013. http://mediamatters.org/research/2008/01/18/ignoring-obamas-statement-on-trumpet-award-hann/142222.

2000. *Saviours Day Jumuah* . Directed by Final Call Publishing. Performed by Imam Warithudeen Mohammed.

2002. *Saviours' Day Jumuah Los Angeles* . Directed by Final Call Publishing. Performed by Imam Warithudeen Mohammed.

Muhammad, Ashahed. 2011. "Farrakhan delivers a warning and offers a healing for spiritual leaders and humanity." *Final Call.com.* May 31. Accessed August 9, 2013. http://www.finalcall.com/artman/publish/National_News_2/article_7872.shtml.

—. 2013. "Farrakhan tells students: You are chosen to build a world!" *Final Call.com.* March 26. Accessed August 10, 2013. http://www.finalcall.com/artman/publish/National_News_2/article_9705.shtml.

—. 2009. "Farrakhan to spiritual leaders: 'God has never done His greatest work in politics'." *Final Call.com.* January 3. Accessed August 9, 2013. http://www.finalcall.com/artman/publish/article_5521.shtml.

—. 2008. "Hip Hop Lives: FCN Interview with Nas." *Final Call.com.* August 4. Accessed August 9, 2013. http://www.finalcall.com/artman/publish/Entertainment_News_5/Hip_Hop_Lives_FCN_Interview_with_Nas_5051.shtml.

—. 2008. "Life and ministry of Imam W. Deen Mohammed remembered." *Final Call.com.* September 21. Accessed August 11, 2013. http://www.finalcall.com/artman/publish/National_News_2/Life_and_ministry_of_Imam_W_Deen_Mohammed_remember_5222.shtml.

Muhammad, Cedric. 2013. "Socialism and Muhammad's Economic Blueprint." *Final Call.com.* August 9. Accessed August 10, 2013. http://www.finalcall.com/artman/publish/Business_amp_Money_12/article_100637.shtml.

Muhammad, Nisa Islam. 2000. "Zionism, not Farrakhan is the problem, rabbis say." *Final Call.com.* March 15. Accessed August 9, 2013. http://www.finalcall.com/national/rabbis2-28-2000.htm.

Muhammad, Starla. 2013. "A man of integrity, consistency and sincerity." *Final Call.com.* May 15. Accessed August 10, 2013.

http://www.finalcall.com/artman/publish/National_News_2/article_9851.shtml.

National Review. 1985. "The Farrakhan Formula." *The National Review*, November 1: 19-20.

O'Reilly, Bill. 2008. "Sticking Up for Rev. Jeremiah Wright and Louis Farrakhan." *Fox News.com.* April 4. Accessed August 10, 2013. http://www.foxnews.com/story/2008/04/04/sticking-up-for-rev-jeremiah-wright-and-louis-farrakhan/.

Osgood, Carl. 1995. "Congressman Disagree on Million Man March." *Executive Intelligence Review*, November 3: 76-77.

Pear, Robert. 1991. "Despite Praising Farrakhan in 1983, Thomas Denies Anti-Semitism." *New York Times*, July 13: 1.7.

Raspberry, William. 1990. "A Visit By Louis Farrakhan." *Washington Post*, May 2: A23.

Rezendes, Michael. 1996. "Muslims' self help praised by Kemp." *Boston Globe*, September 8: A.1.

Sanders, Senator Hank. 2013. "State Senator Supporting Farrakhan's Visit Writes To BJF ." *The Birmingham Jewish Federation.* June 13. Accessed August 10, 2013. http://www.bjf.org/daily-updates/722-state-senator-supporting-farrakhans-visit-writes-to-bjf.html.

Schelzig, Erik. 2009. "Farrakhan: Don't Be "Pacified" By Obama Election." *Huffington Post* . October 19. Accessed August 9, 2013. http://www.huffingtonpost.com/2009/10/19/farrakhan-dont-be-pacifie_n_325616.html.

Simmons, Russell. 2009. *GlobalGrind.com.* September 25. Accessed August 9, 2013. http://globalgrind.com/2009/09/25/minister-louis-farrakhan-my-second-father-2/.

Staff, BET. 2005. "News Person of the Year 2005: Minister Louis Farrakhan." *BET.com.* December 19. Accessed August 10, 2013.

http://www.bet.com/news/news/2008/02/11/newsarticlepersonofyearfarrakhan.html.

Steinberg, Jeffrey. 1995. "March Signals Revolt Against Conservative Revolution." *Executive Intelligence Review*, October 27: 58.

Syed, Ibrahim. n.d. "An International Conference." *Islamic Research Foundation International, Inc.* Accessed August 10, 2013. http://www.irfi.org/articles/articles_51_100/an_international_islamic_confere.htm.

Tabor, Daniel K. 1985. ". . . no, that's not the issue." *Houston Chronicle*, September 18: 11.

The American Prospect. 2002. "Lunatic League Formed." *American Prospect*, March 11: 7.

The Final Call. 1996. "World Friendship Tour Coverage-South Africa." *The Final Call*, February 14.

ThomasJr., Harry L. 1989. "In Praise of Louis Farrakhan: Mr. Thomas Replies." *Washington Post*, October 27: A18.

Wall, James M. 1995. "Message and messenger: the Million Man March." *The Christian Century*, November 1: 1003.

Watson, Jamal E. 2005. "New Amsterdam Interview With President Clinton." *New Amsterdam News*, May 5-11: 1.

Willis, Professor Andre C. 2012. "79 Years Young: A Look at Farrakhan's Legacy." *UrbanCusp.com*. May 11. Accessed August 10, 2013. http://www.urbancusp.com/newspost/79-years-young-a-look-at-farrakhans-legacy/.

Wycliff, Don. 1995. ""Why Farrakhan appeals: touching the souls of black folk."." *Commonweal*, November 17: 8.

Special Thanks

Deep Love and Gratitude to the Honorable Minister Louis Farrakhan for his generosity, love, guidance and support. Love and appreciation to my wife Tomiko and my children. Much Love and Brotherhood to my colleagues in the NOI Research Group. Deep Gratitude to Minister Anthony Muhammad Brother Alan Muhammad, Brother Cedric Muhammad, Brother Jesse Muhammad, Brother Sultan Muhammad and Minister Robert Muhammad. Much Love and Appreciation to my father Sammie and my mother Marilyn. Special Thanks to Brother Michael X Courtney. I received encouragement, advice and brotherhood from some of Minister Farrakhan's dedicated student ministers: Thanks and Appreciation to Minister Don Muhammad(Boston, MA), Minister Tony Muhammad(Los Angeles, CA), Minister Keith Muhammad(Oakland, CA), Minister Christopher Muhammad(San Francisco, CA), Minister James Muhammad(Tampa, FL), Minister Michael Muhammad(Tampa, FL), Minister William Muhammad(Milwaukee, WI), Brother Mark Muhammad (Boston, MA) and Brother Randy Muhammad(Boston, MA).

I would like to also thank Minister Courtney Muhammad of (Utica, NY), Brother Victor Muhammad (Boston, MA), Clyde Muhammad (Memphis, TN) and Brother Minister Jihad Muhammad (Pine Bluff, AR) for material support in the printing of this book. Thanks Sister Landra Muhammad for typing assistance and important transcriptions. Thanks to Brother Seth Muhammad, Sister Victoria Muhammad (Oakland, CA) and Brother Student Captain Mark Muhammad (San Francisco, CA) for important library assistance. Thanks to Brother Hannibal Muhammad (Phoenix, CA) for use of his beautiful photograph of Minister Farrakhan that is used in the cover artwork. Thanks to all of the brother and sisters who encourage our work and express their appreciation for what we are trying to do to help Minister Farrakhan be seen clearly without the hindrance and obstruction of the enemy's propaganda.

Thank You, Thank You, Thank You!

Made in the USA
Middletown, DE
12 August 2022